Praise for What Million-Dollar Brands Know

From beginning to end What Million Dollar Brands Know is the business owner's Global Positioning Strategy, GPS, to success (yes, I took liberty with the S, strategy was more meaningful than system). For me, the tone-setter was "be brilliant in the basics" and the clincher was the questions at the end of each chapter. These reinforced the ideas in the chapter and caused me to think beyond my current situation.

Lisa uncovers the facts many people skip right over in branding: the name, the values and, the promise; and jump to colors and logos as "the brand." Hiring the right people. How they can make or break you. The transparency of the business owner's resilience in the face of betrayal and strategic sabotage. Lisa brings these points and more to life with the examples of successes and challenges business owners have had.

There is no ideal audience; because it is a must-read for all business owners. If you're in the planning stages, you can do it right the first time. Startups can mitigate risk and redirect early. Established business this is your opportunity to rebrand. I will be using these strategies and nuggets with my customers. What Million Dollar Brands Know is the newest tool in my client welcome kit.

Vicki Semander
Owner & Sr. Consultant
Beyond Branding

"This extremely practical and useful book covers all the basics of how to marketing for start-ups and also for those who are rebranding. Lisa includes insights about the value in a name, brand archetypes, defining your target audience, what works best in digital marketing, the value of collaboration and so much more. She's put together a fantastic book with information that gets to the point so that you can get to work."

Cindy K. Hide
Family Law Attorney and Founder of
Love, Money & the Law

What Million-Dollar Brands KN●W

What Million-Dollar Brands KNOW

Marketing & Branding Strategies for Today's Entrepreneur

Lisa N. Alexander
THE MARKETING STYLIST™

ellis valin
COMMUNICATIONS

To every small business owner working towards generating their first million.

CONTENTS

INTRODUCTION

Service providers and product makers all have the same goal, get their product or service in front of the right people.

And how do businesses and brands do that?

Through the time-honored tradition of marketing.

The goal of marketing hasn't changed. However, how we do so, has. With the introduction of social media, digital marketing, marketing automation tools, and AI or artificial intelligence, businesses can put their products and services directly in front of their target audience in ways unheard of just a decade ago.

This new technology can track customers online, generate and target ads that appear on their online spaces and mobile devices. This technology can track how much time customers spend on your website, even specific web pages. There's eye-tracking software and even software that can tell how long customers hover over your *buy now* or *see more* buttons.

Businesses and brands no longer have to wonder what their audience think or spend time sending out lengthy customer surveys. Not when companies like Yelp, Amazon, and Google host millions of product and service reviews. And customer service is no longer regulated to a manned, 9-to-5, 1-800 number. Twitter and other social media platforms remedied that. Customers can publicly lodge complaints twenty-four hours a day, seven days a week on social media, which means you must be ready to respond to issues quickly.

With all the technological marvels and advances marketers and businesses have at their collective fingertips, some tried-and-true methods remain. Mass marketing via direct-response television (DRTV) or product infomercials produces billions of dollars annually and that trend is still growing. According to *The Economics of Infomercials*, growth was expected to "exceed $250 billion as of 2015."

And for all those who prophesied print would surely be dead by now, *31 Essential Direct Mail Marketing Automation Stats You Need to Know* reports that, "90 percent of all direct mail gets opened while only 20-30 percent of all emails get read."

Older methodologies like direct mail and infomercials still work, even if they're not as sexy as Facebook ads or creating electronic advertising fences around physical locations.

I've been in the industry for over two decades at the time of this writing and here's my marketing truth...even though how we market has changed, the basic principles have not. And that's what the million-dollar brands I interviewed understood (which is probably one of the reasons why they're million-dollar brands).

Companies still need to get their products and services seen by their target audiences and get those products and services sold.

I had the good fortune to interview a group of fabulous women business owners—all generating a million dollars or more in their businesses and they shared their marketing truths with me. They own successful daycares, law firms, and consulting businesses. One, manufactures the best peanut butter you'll ever taste and another, alcoholic beverages to help with any inhibitions you might want to shed.

What do million-dollar brands know? They know that even though marketing tools and technology change, you can't run from the basics. They know that a fancy logo and color standard guide and a slew of ads on Facebook are not the geneses of a million-dollar brand.

These businesses and brands mastered the marketing basics—the who and the what before ever attempting the how.

New business owners can often get caught up in what I call the *Shiny New Object Syndrome*—i.e. the newest marketing tool that is guaranteed to deliver customers and sales fast. As a consultant, I've witnessed far too many entrepreneurs spend thousands of dollars on the latest marketing gadgets and overnight marketing gurus without giving the time, thought or attention to the basics.

They might have had a lovely logo with a semi-functioning website but again, not much thought to who they were marketing to and fine-tuning the product or service they deliver to the marketplace.

I remember the first time I heard someone say, "Be brilliant in the basics." It struck me because no one wants to be basic. Entrepreneurs and business owners strive to be anything but and pay handsomely to appear so.

But mastering the marketing basics is what sets these million-dollar brands apart from the rest. When you master this, you weave that knowledge into 'the how' and create successful campaigns that get you to your goal: money-spending, content-sharing, positive-review-giving, repeat customers.

ACKNOWLEDGMENTS

An undertaking of this magnitude is not a one-woman mission! Trust me it is not. I am forever grateful for my National Association of Women Business Owner (NAWBO) sister and national program director, Lynda Bishop for her help with this project! Lynda, thank you! I'll see you at National!

To all the fabulous women business owners who said yes to the interview and took the time to chat with me, thank you. I appreciate your thoughtfulness and consideration of the subject matter and sharing your expertise. Your words of wisdom will influence many!

So to, Limaris Alvarado of Echo Consulting, Jessica Billingsley of MJ Freeway, Jennifer Breen of SuiteHome, Marcelle Flower of Armstrong Plumbing, Loreen Gilbert of WealthWise Financial Services, Jill Kerrigan of JAK

Design, Merrilee Kick of Southern Champion, Nancy Klensch of Summit Kids, Vicki LaRose of Civil Design, Inc., Kristi Mirambell of K-Belle Consultants, Lisa Scott of Scott Global Migration Law Group, Anne Staines of Sagent Marketing, Anne Trompeter of Live Marketing, Biddie Webb of LIMB Design, Kimmi Wernli of Crazy Richard's Peanut Butter, Laura Yamanaka of Team CFO, a world of thanks to you all.

To the group of business owners who said yes and took part in my initial focus group, thank you! Errol Allen of Errol Allen Consulting, Sharee Johnson-Cammon of The B.A.M. Market, Lara Mfon of Vital Woman Magazine, Bridget Fizer of Meaningful Life with Dr. Bridget Fizer, Catherine Hoyem of Empower the Change and Markita Samuels of Making Straight Paths, you all are the best! Thank you for your input, your critiques and most of all your support and love. I appreciate all of you.

To my family, thank you for your patience and understanding while I stayed tethered to my desk to complete this project. We are all due a vacation!

Finally, to the man who keeps me grounded, won't let me settle for less and has been my biggest cheerleader since day one, my beloved husband Elgin. When life got crazy, you let me rest but wouldn't let me stop. Thank you. Thanks for believing in me and supporting me. I will love you always.

CHAPTER ONE
Alas, What's in a Name?

"You can greatly reduce the long-term costs of your [marketing] campaign if your name and your brand positioning and your brand promise are in alignment with what the company does."

-Anne Staines, Sagent Marketing

One of my favorite things to do is to help clients develop their brand. I promise I love this process. Helping clients choose their name, determine their values and establish their brand definition and promise is a journey I thoroughly enjoy. Defining the company culture and how interactions happen online and offline—

between employees and management, management and suppliers is a challenge I find utterly rewarding. I love the process of helping clients build their target audience avatars and then see it all come to life in the visual identities created. I equate it to starting with a patch of dirt and seeing a 10,000 sq. ft. box retail store emerge. Out of nothing, the client and I create something amazing! It wasn't there before but now, a living, breathing entity that reflects everything my client has dreamed exists. This ladies and gentlemen never gets old.

Choosing a name for a business, book or event can be a very sensitive and personal matter. Sometimes, not much thought is given to this very critical building block of a brand.

Sagent Marketing President and Chief Strategist, Anne Staines shared this about naming your business:

> *"One of the companies we're working with came up with a name for a new product off the top of their head. The name they selected didn't evoke something positive and did not align with SEO terms for their industry.*
>
> *So, can we create a brand around that? We can. Nike did it with a name that meant nothing to most people. But how much easier would it be if the name popped up easily on an SEO term when*

*people are organically looking for what they want?
How much easier would it be if we're not having to
overcome initial questions of,* 'that doesn't sound
very good or very positive.'

*So, spending dollars upfront to do real branding
research and to measure how much natural
attraction and affinity the name has—it sounds
like a big expense but it's also a big investment for
the longer-term reducing your marketing costs."*

What's in a name? Potentially, a big chunk of your
marketing budget. Your brand name could lead you down
a road to profitability or an endless money pit. Possibly
spending thousands or more explaining to your target
audience who you are and what you do.

OVERSTOCK.COM

Overstock.com is an online retailer selling everything
from clothing to furniture and pretty much everything in
between. According to Wikipedia, when the company was
founded in 1997, it exclusively sold surplus and returned
merchandise on an online e-commerce marketplace. They
liquidated the inventories of at least 18 failed dot com
companies at below wholesale prices.

Twenty years later the company's name no longer
fits. There are far fewer failed dot coms providing an

influx of merchandise for the company to sell. Now, they presumably spend millions of dollars on TV ads and other media explaining how their name no longer adequately describes their business.

One of their commercials is set in an airport with a well-dressed male passenger having an encounter with an airline agent. She reviews his ticket and asks if his name is Oscar La Vista. She laughs and amends Arnold Schwarzenegger's line from the movie Terminator 2, "Oscar La Vista, baby" and laughs hysterically. The narrator then explains how getting judged on your name is tough.

And costly.

Think it's just business names that can confuse your customer?

Not even.

The name of your event can also draw or repel your target audience and impact whether you'll sell out, or go home empty-handed. The wrong name can bring you an audience you never intended.

Product names also matter. Your book title matters.

I remember one potential client was adamant on a book title that was way too long. Nine-to-ten words if I remember correctly. It was ambiguous and gave the reader no reason to pick it up. While they were shocked that sales didn't extend past family and friends, I was not.

When choosing a name, you want to pick a name (include a clear tagline if you must) that makes it clear what you do and what you offer.

Think about how your company may grow and expand. Does that name allow for that growth? Or will you find yourself having to rebrand in a few years? Rebranding isn't a bad thing, but it can be costly. Budgeting for research and testing of a business name on the front end is well worth the initial investment. Just like Anne said.

USING YOUR NAME AS YOUR BUSINESS NAME

Loreen Gilbert of WealthWise Financial Services shared the following:

> *"I was very thoughtful early on when it came to naming my business. Most of the people in my industry used their name in the title of their company. I knew early on I did not want that. I wanted this company to outlive me. And it wasn't going to do that with my name on it or if it did it would become obsolete. No one would know who that was and ask who cares? For me, it was more about making sure that I had a great brand that explained the values that we hold. That the name could be used for generations to come.*

A good colleague of mine regrets that he used his name in his business. Many people do after the fact. So, I tell people to give serious thought about their business name because it's crucial. Some do so for posterity's sake but I thought long and hard about our purpose. We exist to help clients be wise with their money and that's how I came up with the name WealthWise. We help people make wise decisions with the resources that they have."

THE LUPUS WELLNESS MENTOR

When Grace (not her real name) was referred to me, she introduced herself as a health and wellness coach. She wasn't happy with her original logo design and asked if I could create something more fitting. We talked and I learned that Grace was a 30-year lupus survivor. She was preparing to launch her business after retirement because she had witnessed first-hand the unfortunate discrimination that occurs when you reveal such an illness to employers.

I was prepared to create a new logo for her, but I knew a new logo wouldn't fix a branding issue. The business name wasn't reflective of her passion and mission or what she truly wanted to bring to the marketplace.

A week later, I called Grace and suggested that her

current direction would not likely serve her well after she retired. I told her a new logo wouldn't solve the real issue. What she had was an identity crisis and a business name that reflected that crisis.

We spent a number of hours on the phone dissecting her purpose and mission. We were turning her vision into a tangible, viable business. One that she could successfully bring to market when the time was right. After lots of work, The Lupus Lounge™ was created.

You see, after my initial conversation with Grace, it was evident to me that she wasn't a health and fitness coach. She had survived a debilitating illness for over 30 years. She knew the importance of diet and exercise. She had a plethora of information about drug therapies and how to counteract certain side effects. She could show other women living with autoimmune diseases how to thrive.

But the health and fitness coach model was the only option or label she knew. I was able to find her 'blue ocean' and we renamed her business and created the title Lupus Wellness Mentor™. With this new name, there would be no guessing what she did and who she served.

THE BUZZBALLZ STORY

Merrilee Kick of Southern Champion had lots to say about finding the right name for your business.

"I think the name of your product or service is very crucial.

I have a product called BuzzBallz. And as the name suggests, it's an alcoholic beverage in ball-shaped containers that get you buzzed. They're small and cute! It makes people want to pick it up and look at it and hold it in their hand. The name sounds like what the product is, so people remember it.

If you have a weird name like Google or TiVo or Nike, you'll have to spend a bunch of marketing money to help people understand the product or service. When you think of a company with the name Taco Time, very little needs to be explained. You know its probably time to eat a taco somewhere. So, I think the brand name is important.

BuzzBallz wasn't our original brand name. We started with Tropic Chillerz, which was inspired by one of our top products.

The reason we used the name initially was that we're in Texas which is considered the 'Bible Belt.' And one of my distributors suggested people in the 'Bible Belt' wouldn't like the word 'buzz.' He associated it with getting drunk and tried to convince me that wasn't what I wanted to convey.

My response to him was, "Yeah, I do!"

People are drinking the product to get a buzz and to help them relax. That's the truth behind it. You can mask it, hide it or fake it, but the bottom line is they're drinking to get a buzz. It makes them feel good.

They're not drinking because they're thinking of the tropics. That's why we changed our name to BuzzBallz.

So, make naming your business is super important. Otherwise, go ahead and make plans to spend a whole bunch of money on marketing if you have a unique name."

Million-dollar brands know that choosing the right name for a product or service, (events and books, too), can save you plenty of marketing dollars down the line. It can keep you from confusing your customer and help those customers easily find you when conducting an online search.

MILLION-DOLLAR QUESTIONS

- Is my business name, product name, book title or event name memorable?

- Can the product or service offered be determined by the name?

- Did you use your name for your business name? Any regrets?

- Do you agree or disagree with Loreen Gilbert on not using your name?

- After you tell people your business name, do you have to follow-up with a lengthy detailed explanation?

CHAPTER TWO

To Thine Own Self Be True: Why Defining Your Company's Vision, Mission & Personality Matters

B uilding a million-dollar brand that not only survives but thrives past its founder(s), requires the utmost clarity on your brand's purpose. Spending time developing your mission, vision, purpose, and goals is at the very heart of a thriving and profitable brand.

Taking time to develop your brand's core values on the front-end will save you time and resources on the back-end. You will want to predetermine and define your company culture and not have it defined you by employees who may not have your company's best interest at heart.

When you take the time and invest in building these values, they become your *North Star*. They guide you in your interactions with vendors, your customers, and most important, your greatest resource—your employees.

These values will guide you on what to pursue and what opportunities to let pass. Knowing your values and having a well-thought-out mission statement keeps you from wasting time and money on things that don't align with your values or mission. They keep your sails pointed toward your goal and keeps you from veering off course.

These seemingly trivial items (trust me they are not) are what all good brands are built upon. As murky as the entrepreneurial waters can be, setting your values and defining your mission are building blocks you don't want to overlook.

These values trickle down and weave their way into every facet of your business. Even your marketing.

According to Civil Design President, Vicki LaRose, an added benefit of getting clear on the brand's mission and purpose was writing better recruitment ads. It helped her tell a good story.

Her recommendation?

> *"You have to know your mission statement, and your value, so then you have a story to tell. In 2007, we had a big shake-up and I hired somebody to sit down with us to help us figure out our values and they are values we still hold today. That's when the company culture we designed started to manifest.*
>
> *If somebody hasn't done that, they need to sit down*

after they've been around a little bit to figure out their values. By doing so, it will help them tell their story and makes marketing easy because they have a story to tell. You have to know your mission."

GROWTH HAPPENS WHEN VALUES AND CULTURE ARE DEFINED AND APPLIED

Marcelle Flower of Armstrong Plumbing shared her company's growth story and attributes it to holding fast to the company's five core values: caring, professional, team, integrity and inspire.

"We've been at this about seven years and we've grown quite quickly. From $1.5 million to $7 million. Our advertising budget has always run around 1.5 percent, and we've kept to this small budget from the company's inception.

I've been asked how we grew so fast and I believe it's because not only did we apply our culture internally but externally to our customers as well.

We have five core values that our team created: caring, professional, team, integrity and inspire. To us, the most important is caring.

My competitors do a lot of this too, but we go the extra mile in making sure the experience is just perfect. If my customers do not have a great experience, then we owe them another one. This approach has resulted in an 88% customer retention rate. We carry our company's culture into the customer's home, and I believe that customers sense that and that's my goal.

We've taken part of our marketing budget and applied it to the customers we serve and have seen an instant return."

WHAT HAPPENS WHEN YOU FAIL TO DEFINE YOUR CULTURE?

Failing to define a company or organization's culture can cost significantly. It can cost you revenue, market share or your business altogether.

So what is culture? Simply stated, it's what a company believes and how they choose to behave. I tell my clients company culture is how you answer the phone, it's how you interact on and offline with your customers. Company culture is reflected through dress codes, business décor, business hours, even hiring decisions.

And, you don't have to be the size of Microsoft or Zappos to define culture. Small businesses and entrepreneurs can and should define their culture too.

Before Shaun King was a well-known civil rights

activist, he was the founder and pastor of a church in Atlanta called Courageous Church. He resigned three years after the church opened.

After the dust settled, he wrote about the experience on ChurchLeaders.com. There he shared what he'd learned.

One of his reasons had everything to do with culture and his failure to define it and implement it at the church's inception. He was then unable to course-correct the trajectory the church had taken. The culture had already been defined and the stakeholders did not buy into his vision or values.

In his post, he encouraged leaders to start their organization exactly how they envisioned. You see, King is an avid do-gooder: fights social injustices, and cares for and empowers the marginalized in his community and abroad. However, he failed to incorporate those values and admitted he started an organization that was primarily focused on the Sunday morning experience. He confessed that he created a super cool Sunday experience to gain attendance and spent three years trying to build the church he originally imagined.

King's advice? "Whatever it is you are starting (a business, a new job, a church, etc.), you need to remain as true to your core vision from the start as humanly possible, or you may find yourself lost in an unfamiliar place so far from your dream that you don't even recognize it."

I agree with King. It's far better to set your company's culture at the start then try to course correct later.

As in LaRose's case, she invited her whole team to help determine what the company's values and goals should be. And according to company culture expert, Melissa Porterfield of Silk Mountain Solutions, bringing employees into the process is the best. She highlights an experience where the founder does exactly that.

> *"A software start-up learned about company culture the hard way. They had abruptly changed direction and the change had been handled poorly. It had been announced in an all-hands meeting, but the "why" behind it hadn't been communicated.*

> *Almost immediately employees started leaving and the remaining employees were angry and confused. They viewed the new direction almost as an affront. They hadn't known anything about it and here it was with no compelling explanation.*

> *I was brought in to stem the flow of exiting employees and after one conversation saw that the company had a serious culture problem.*

> *The CEO worked on a vision statement that was*

clear and compelling. It had to explain why the company existed. Ultimately, he decided "We give your data wings," but without knowing how to give your data wings, it was just words.

In another all-hands, he rolled out the vision and explained that it now needed a mission and values to support it. He told the employees that he wanted their help and got a lukewarm reception. Only five of the 50 employees volunteered.

Those five people were enough to start the process. As we worked on the mission statement, we began to create some buzz and more employees wanted to be included. As the group got bigger, we had to split into smaller groups and then come back together to agree on results. The debates were passionate at times, but in the end, all agreed.

Ultimately, the mission statement was, "To breathe new life into your data with XXX". The employees proudly presented it to the leadership team, and they loved it.

Encouraged, the groups tackled the company values. This was harder as all had to agree to abide by them, no matter what (especially leadership).

After much discussion, they came up with three they felt exemplified what they wanted to be known for:

- *Be the example*
- *Share your brilliance*
- *Care*

When they went back to the leadership team to present their final product, the team was blown away (I had kept the CEO in the loop, but he hadn't said a word to anyone.)

When the CEO had his third all-hands, you could tell the atmosphere had changed into one of anticipation. The employees that had participated got to roll it out, which they did with much enthusiasm, and while there was still some skepticism in the room, overall it was very positive.

You'd think that was the end of the story. It wasn't. While the creation process had been hard, keeping a culture alive and well is even harder. You must keep the communication flowing, you must be accountable and most difficult of all, you may have to let some go. It takes commitment.

Culture can be an intangible thing, but when you walk into that office, you can feel it."

CULTURE AND EXPANSION

Million-dollar brand owner, Lisa Scott of Scott Global Migration Law Group learned about culture after she was ready to scale her business. She downsized her business as a single mother but after her daughter started high school, she was ready to expand. She credits a program called ScaleUp offered by the Small Business Administration (SBA) and facilitated by the Women's Business Development Center.

While in that program she understood that she wasn't just a lawyer, but a business owner and she had never thought of herself in that way. She also understood that she could no longer joke and say, "I make money despite my efforts." Now Scott is making money because of her efforts.

The ScaleUp program also helped Scott to think differently about her role in her company. "I thought that I was the boss and that was it. But if I wanted to be effective, I needed to be the leader and that's very different," Scott said.

She also learned that defining culture was key.

> *"In leading, I realized that I can teach people how to do immigration, but I couldn't teach them how to fit into our team. You have to hire for the culture. And I had to ask, well what is my culture?*

I discovered that mine is a little different. I don't fit into the corporate culture and could never fit into that environment. I had to determine what was important to us as a company. And for us, it was customer service.

When we started recruiting, not only did we look for people with a bachelor's degree, but we wanted to know if they worked retail during high school. Because I wanted to hire people who knew about time management and who knew what money was about—people who knew how it felt to spend their own money.

We recently hired three people and when I asked why they responded to our ad, they said because the ad was intriguing. They said our ad explained what we were looking for, who we were as a company and the kind of person who would fit in the company. We got some great fits and yes, we're struggling to teach them how to do immigration but at 6 PM on a Friday, we were all standing around joking when the office closes at five. That told me that culture was super important. So, we knew members of the 5:05 club, you know when it's 5 PM and they're out the door, those people aren't a good fit for our company.

If you place one of those boring ads that say, "legal assistant, bachelor's degree, experience preferred, foreign language required" you're not always going to get someone who fits your company's culture. We said things like, "we don't always wear shoes that match, we love dogs and bring them to the office, we never take no for an answer, we worked jobs in high school" and we got some amazing responses from placing an ad based on our culture; not just the job requirements.

In our office, we have one big table and we call it the "News Room." It reminded me of some movie I watched where everybody stood around a big table talking. So, this huge table is our hub. You can stand or sit around this table.

One morning, I noticed that we were all seated and it was very quiet, and everyone was very focused. You could look up at any moment and yes, there'd be someone in front of you or right next to you, but everyone was in their zone. Now some people do wear headphones, but I can tune out anything!

One person asked a question and people got involved in the conversation and shared their experiences and how they solved the problem previously. This setup encourages collaboration.

When I was in school and had to work in teams, I hated it because there was always that one slacker. I couldn't stand teamwork, but I understand that now it's the wave of the future. It will be about working collaboratively and this is the culture we've defined for ourself."

MILLION-DOLLAR QUESTIONS

- Have you defined your company's mission and value?

- If you've done so, how has this impacted your business? Your marketing?

- Have you defined your company culture?

- Are your company values and the customer experience in harmony?

CHAPTER THREE
Branding, Culture and Customer Service

"If you as the owner illustrate or model good customer service, then I think it spreads through the company faster than anything else."

Vicki LaRose, Civil Design, Inc.

One of my favorite things to do is help entrepreneurs develop their brand. It's an opportunity I don't take lightly! Together we bring their vision and their dream to life. This process never gets old! Once we establish brand definitions and promises, once we talk target audience and visual identities, and talk about the brand's mission and core values, we have a conversation about culture and customer service.

You might think these three things are separate functions, but they are not. They are all tied and the business that understands this is a business with happy employees, vendors, customers, and a healthy bottom line.

WHAT IS BRANDING?

If you ask someone to explain branding, I can assure you'll get a variety of answers. Some will say that your logo is your brand and I've always disagreed with the simplicity of that answer.

Your logo may be the visual representation of your brand but by itself, it is not your brand. When done correctly, your mark can come to symbolize everything your brand stands for but there's a process to make that happen.

My definition of branding is this; it is the how and why a person, business, product or service shows up in the marketplace. This ladies and gentlemen is what separates or differentiates you from everyone else in the marketplace. It is the very beginnings of establishing a successful, recognizable brand.

If your customers agree with your *why* and *how*, congratulations. You have a functioning brand. If your customers don't agree, then we have what's called brand confusion and that can be costly to rectify.

There are a variety of ways to position yourself in the marketplace. You can be a corporate brand, luxury brand, personal brand, product brand or celebrity brand.

In the end, all businesses fall under one of the 12 Brand Archetypes:

- The Innocent - wants to be happy
- The Regular Guy or Gal - wants to belong
- The Hero - wants to prove themselves
- The Outlaw - wants a revolution
- The Explorer - wants freedom
- The Creator - wants perfection
- The Ruler - wants absolute power
- The Magician - wants to make dreams come true
- The Lover - wants to indulge you
- The Caregiver - wants to nurture
- The Jester - wants to make you laugh/free-spirited
- The Sage - wants the truth

Merrilee Kick of Southern Champion describes brand archetypes as personalities. According to Kick, to be successful, a business needs to identify this early on.

> *"Your brand has a personality and you have to make sure that your social media channels and your website reflects that personality.*
>
> *You have to ask, is it a party brand or a fun brand? Is it colorful or very serious? Is it relaxed or rough? Brands have a personality just like people."*

Fellow marketer and branding expert, Denise Lee Yohn developed her list of brand types to identify general approaches to brand positioning that correspond to values in an organization's culture. Her list includes the:

1. Disruptive Brand — Challenges the current ways of doing things and introduces new concepts that substantively change the market

2. Conscious Brand — Is on a mission to make a positive social or environmental impact or enhance people's quality of life

3. Service Brand — Consistently delivers high-quality customer care and service

4. Innovative Brand — Consistently introduces advanced and breakthrough products and technologies

5. Value Brand — Offers lower prices for basic quality

6. Performance Brand — Offers products that deliver superior performance and dependability

7. Luxury Brand — Offers higher quality at a higher price

8. Style Brand — Is differentiated through the way its products or services look and feel, as much as or more than what they do

9. Experience Brand — Is differentiated through the experience it provides, as much as or more than the product or service.

Determine the kind of brand you want to be. This will guide you in how you show up in the marketplace.

BRANDING AND COMPANY CULTURE

Zappos has long been the poster child for company culture and branding done right. Ask any Zappos customer, employee or supplier and they will more than likely sing the company's praises. The founder, Tony Hsieh, was intentional from the beginning of developing a brand and culture that created an environment for all to thrive.

Uber, unfortunately, is the poster child for company culture gone wrong. With allegations and reports of sexual harassment, bullying, and retaliation, Uber—a couple of CEOs later—is making strides in changing that culture.

Setting Company Culture Needs to Be Intentional

When you're designing your logo and picking out colors, that's the time to decide on your company's culture. It's one of the things you don't want to leave to chance.

Uber never had a written policy that specifically said

to harass women employees and never allow them to advance within the company. (At least I hope not!) This hostile culture, according to former Uber engineer, Susan Fowler, in her infamous blog post titled, *One Very, Very Strange Year at Uber*, was built on behavior demonstrated by those in top management positions. Online, it was described as the open secret everyone knew about. This bad behavior was not only tolerated but celebrated.

You see, company culture is what is done by those in top leadership positions and those behaviors are adopted and understood as normal throughout the organization. Company culture has to be embraced and demonstrated by all. It can't be a set of values on posters.

Every company has a culture but not all company culture is purposefully built. Companies that do not intentionally build a healthy work culture or go through a radical change such as a merger, spend hundreds of thousands of dollars on change management experts.

Million-dollar brands know that well-defined company cultures can create a thriving work environment.

Build the Culture and Like the People You Work With

For Jessica Billingsley of MJ Freeway, establishing the company culture resulted in hiring people who rally around their core values. The bonus was these people enjoyed being around each other and made for great office morale.

> *"I wanted to create a culture where I like the people and I want to work with them every day.*
>
> *When you get that first thing right by hiring the right people, you end up with amazing people on your team. Then you're committed to keeping those hiring standards high so that you can continue to foster the right culture."*

Company Culture Can Create Raving Fans

Billingsley also said that being intentional with building company culture makes it easy for customers to become fans.

> *"For us, it starts with culture and when you get the culture right and that culture is communicated to your clients, that's how you get raving fans. That's how you get people that feel like they're a part of your company or even say, "Hey, I want to come work for you someday."*

BRANDING AND CUSTOMER SERVICE

I tell my clients that not only is branding reflected in your new logo and website, but it's also reflected in how you answer the phone. It's reflected in how you interact with clients on and offline. Do those encounters live up to your brand message and definition?

Customer service expert, Errol Allen chatted on my podcast back in 2014 on this very subject. He said that customer service not only reflects the strength of your brand and culture, it also impacts your bottom line.

Jennifer Breen of SuiteHome agrees.

> *"In our business, we have a one-hour turnaround time. Requests and inquiries are always responded to within the hour. Customer service makes and breaks you at this point. It's the biggest differentiator in my industry."*

Customer Service Plus Culture Equals Customer Retention

During my interview with Marcelle Flower of Armstrong Plumbing, she said that it was not uncommon for her team to take the trash out for clients or buy treats for a customer's pet to show clients that they cared. It's those little things that make a brand stand out and makes the brand experience memorable.

Concerning keeping customers happy, Flower says, "We applied our culture to our customers."

She went on to say:

> *"I want her [the customer] for life so I spend a lot of my money saving her rather than spending an*

exorbitant amount trying to get new customers. I want to keep her because she's my biggest mouthpiece. She's going to go tell her neighbors about us next time she's in the supermarket."

Armstrong Plumbing has a dedicated task force that works on customer retention. According to Flower, this task force can turn around 95 percent of those who said they had a bad experience. In the end, those customers turn out to be the best referrals and the loudest mouthpieces for the company.

LaRose of Civil Design, Inc. so values customer service that new hires don't interact with clients immediately. She says:

"If your people aren't courteous and ready to help solve problems, you've got to coach them and make sure they're ready to speak to a client. [In our company] there's a certain level you have to reach before you get to speak to a client. Make sure that your people are ready and have the right words. And even with emails, you have to make sure they're using the right words. With every email, you're touching the client and you want to make sure they are saying what you want them to say."

"In our business, everybody markets even though they may not know it. We've got to teach our

younger people they're marketing no matter what they're doing."

The Rewards of Good Customer Service

Kathryn Freeland of A-TEK doesn't just seek to satisfy her customers, she and her team aim to delight them. To Freeland and her team that means "not only delivering what we promised in our proposal but how can we go over and beyond to make the client look good?"

She further explains:

> *"So how do we delight them? How do we become important to their organization? How do we make it so that they can't live without us? That they can't function without us. They can't move their vision forward without us. How do we become so ingrained within their organization that we are seen as critical components to the success of their organization? That's the ultimate in customer satisfaction right there."*

"Cheaper to Keep Her" — Customer Retention

It's common wisdom that keeping a customer is less expensive than acquiring a new one. So, making sure customers and employees are happy and employees have the skills and training needed to take care of customers is of great importance.

Freeland went on to say that retention is done daily. She says that they "can't take any customer for granted." According to Freeland, customers "can be in love with us today and they can be out of love with us tomorrow because someone new came in and offered them better."

So, how do she and her team stay connected to customers?

> "Quarterly, I conduct what I call quality service visits to our customers. It's part of my retention strategy as CEO. So from my position to the help desk person that's delivering the service, we all have a responsibility for maintaining and retaining these relationships. Such that they want to not only continue to work with us on current work, but they see the value we bring to their organization and want to work with us on a long-term basis.

> From a marketing standpoint, it's tied to what they contracted us do, but also, what additional value we can bring to them as we learn about each other. And what our customers learn is that they don't have to pigeonhole us into any one category."

MILLION-DOLLAR QUESTIONS

- What kind of environment do you want to create for you and your team?

- How should team members and vendors interact?

- How should team members and customers interact?

- What values do you want to be represented in your company?

- How are those demonstrated by your team?

- How do you integrate social consciousness into your company culture and brand?

Remember your company culture and brand isn't a set it once and done event. You should revisit and assess regularly.

CHAPTER FOUR
Knowing Your Target Audience

"I don't believe you need to be something to everyone because if you're marketing to everyone, you're marketing to no one. Nobody is going to pick up on what you're trying to convey."

-Nancy Klensch, Summit Kids

"You need to know your demographic, and you won't usually know until after you get it out there. Then, you start figuring out who's buying, start delving into it and asking them questions."

-Merrilee Kick, Southern Champion

Years ago, I was part of a Facebook group for entrepreneurs and business owners and encountered a man we'll call Eric—Eric the Mechanic. Eric posted photos of work he'd done for a customer and the great reviews he received.

A fellow group member was impressed and asked Eric the Mechanic about his target audience to refer potential customers to his business. Eric the Mechanic said the words that make every marketer cringe, "Everybody! Everybody is my customer!" I wanted to reach through my computer to shake him and scream no. You don't want everybody as your customer! I promise you that you do not.

KNOWING YOUR AUDIENCE'S PAIN POINTS AND CREATING SOLUTIONS

"Know your role in their life and that you're fixing a problem for them. Know that you're enhancing their life in some way. Know what your product or service is doing for that person."

-Nancy Klensch, Summit Kids

Humans are complicated beings who experience a wide range of emotions. We feel excited when a favorite team wins a big game or when the youngest child finally gets potty trained. We feel sad when we lose a loved one or get laid off from a job. We feel a sense of relief when we finally pay off a debt or get a favorable answer to a request. We experience a variety of feelings and marketers look for ways to marry products and services to the feelings of potential customers.

Consider the messages that show wide-eyed puppies in kennels or orphaned sea lions with melodramatic music playing that pull on heartstrings during the holidays. This type of messaging appeals to the compassion and generosity most feel during this time of year and it works.

Klensch has successfully pinpointed her target audiences greatest pain point and the emotion attached to it…GUILT! Her team knows that many moms feel guilty about having to leave their kids at daycare.

> *"Our target audience is families with working parents. When these parents go to work and they have to put their kids in childcare; they feel guilty. The number one thing they feel is guilt. Whatever pain they might feel about having to pay for the service is always overshadowed by the guilt.*

> *Working moms often battle thoughts like, "If I could only be at home with my kid." My goal is to have moms not feel guilty. I want parents to feel just as good about dropping their kids off at our center as if they were sending their kid to a private school.*

> *And parents brag about that, right? "Oh, my kid*

goes to private school and I pay X amount." We brag about how much we pay when it comes to private school, but when it comes to childcare, all of a sudden there's shame. Not to mention, running into that one super mom who doesn't work outside the home.

So our first goal is to help alleviate parent guilt. I want parents to know that their children are in good hands. That their child's happiness and growth will thrive. I want parents to feel just as good dropping them off with us as they would dropping them off at grandma's house."

LISTENING AND LEARNING FROM YOUR TARGET AUDIENCE

Years ago, I was brought in on the very beginning stages of a big project. The company was a long-time client of the consultant who hired me, but this particular business center was going to be a new client.

During our very first meeting, my role was to listen, take notes and observe. Things happened at that meeting that would forever impact how I conducted meetings with potential clients.

Strike One: The Poorly Scheduled Money Meeting

The meeting was scheduled for 4 PM on a Friday and one of the meeting attendees let us know this was a bad idea from the moment we sat down at the table. He repeatedly stated that Friday's were the one day of the week he was responsible for picking up his little girl and taking her to an after school event. Was this brought up before the meeting was confirmed? I don't know. But I did question if Friday at 4 PM was ever a good time to schedule a money meeting.

I do know that the consultant didn't have this key player's attention or his support. He spent the entire meeting looking at his watch and checking his phone. He was impatient and his body language said so. The consultant plowed forward regardless.

What do you do at this moment? Since more than one key player attended the meeting, he could have been excused and called in from the road which would have exhibited understanding. Or the most senior manager could have easily handled the meeting and filled his colleague in later. The lesson here is to be flexible enough to pivot in real-time. Anything would have been better than to continue a meeting with a decision-maker whose feathers were ruffled by a poorly timed meeting because.

Strike Two: Holding Critical Information Hostage

As I watched interest wane and frustration grow, the

unthinkable happened. The consultant was going through their presentation when one of the decision-makers quite bluntly asked for the numbers. The consultant told him that they had not gotten to that point in the presentation and that he would have to wait.

I was horrified and hoped my poker face was still holding. All the while I'm thinking, does this consultant want this contract or not?

This was the reason we were here—to talk numbers. To my amazement, the consultant didn't have a single number to present. They were simply rehashing information from a previous meeting.

I know this because the most senior decision-maker said so. I couldn't believe what I was witnessing. Did this consultant just tell a potential client that they would have to wait and then not have the information they were expecting? Why yes. Yes, they did.

What should you do at this moment? This may seem simple but be prepared! Give the client what they asked for! Deliver on your promise. If you schedule a money meeting, be ready to talk money, especially if it's 4 PM on a Friday. Be ready to talk value. Be ready to talk deliverables. Don't waste the client's time by rehashing the obvious. Now, the decision-maker who is late picking up his little girl is incensed. Not only is he late; now he's not even getting the information promised.

Strike Three: Not Listening and Taking Clients for Granted

Because this consultant serviced several business centers within the company, they made the mistake of not listening to this potential client. They leaned heavily on their overall familiarity of the business and brushed off legitimate concerns they had.

The consultant then made the grave mistake of not taking their concerns about falling oil prices seriously. They were being extremely cautious, and that is why they were willing to meet on a Friday at 4 PM. They wanted to know if this project was something they could move forward on or if they should put on hold.

My advice to any business owner is to listen. Don't speculate or second-guess what the client is telling you and certainly don't dismiss their concerns. If they say they are concerned about something happening in the marketplace; address it, suggest alternate options and provide 'if-this-then-that' solutions.

As the consultant and I stood in the parking lot recapping the meeting, they seemed completely surprised by it all. They reiterated how ridiculous the falling oil price concerns were and left there assured that they would close the deal. They were appalled by the dad missing his little girl's behavior and thought his rudeness and brashness was uncalled for. They were certain they'd close the deal and the project would get underway in a matter of months.

I got in my car and wondered if we had just attended the same meeting because my takeaway was completely different.

For me, that whole meeting reaffirmed that:

- You give clients what they ask for, not what you think they should have.

- Be ready to pivot and adjust in real-time.

- Listening and delivering on your promises are still skills that increase your company's revenue.

- Showing a little empathy/compassion can gain you a much-needed business ally.

DOING BUSINESS WITH NON-TARGET AUDIENCE MEMBERS

I'm sure Eric The Mechanic eventually learned that no everyone was his ideal customer. Every business owner eventually learns this lesson. Laura Yamanaka, of TeamCFO, says that "selling to anybody who wants your service can end up being an experience that does not go well." She learned that some business owners will have a case of sticker shock because they've never worked with a senior financial person before."

Here's what else Yamanaka learned.

"I came out of corporate so, I knew all about defining my target audience and creating my mission statement and focusing on selling to the right people. But when you first start your business, you think that somehow you could still make money.

You know this is a bad idea intellectually, but you get so excited about the sale and you're thrilled that someone wants to work with you. You're excited someone said yes.

But then I quickly realized that there was a reason why we said we wouldn't initially work with startups. Unless they were serious entrepreneurs, they didn't understand the difference between a CFO and a bookkeeper. They wanted to know why we were so expensive compared to the others.

I learned that when working with people outside of my target audience I need to be very clear about the cost upfront. By doing so, I eliminate the questions why I'm not making money six months into the project and why am I mad at this client, and why are they mad at me? You have to make these judgment calls before you take on the client."

WHEN THE FEDERAL GOVERNMENT IS YOUR TARGET AUDIENCE

I hope that while reading this book, you discover that companies market to their target audience in different ways. The companies featured so far have ranged from childcare centers to hospitality to professional services. So it should come as no surprise then, marketing to the government is going to be different than marketing to your average consumer. This is B2B marketing on steroids. Kathryn Freeland of A-TEK shares her process.

> *"The federal government is such a broad industry, so we have to narrow it down. Our customer is not the federal government per se, it is a specific agency within the federal government—even a specific department.*
>
> *It's a matter of drilling down to identify the customer and audience that you're initially targeting to determine what the client needs and how to marketing to that customer.*
>
> *And even though our services may apply to the broader federal government, there's no way one company can market to the entire federal government. It's just impossible. So, it is important to understand that audience, their mission, their*

objectives, their vision. What keeps them up at night? What is it that they're looking for – what are the tools and systems and things that they need to achieve their objectives and how does your offering meet those needs?

So, not only do we try to understand them at a deeper level but then how do you use your products, service, whatever it is that you are selling to help solve their problem? And so, by understanding that audience, knowing what their problems are, then we can better tailor our tools, our systems, our services to help meet their needs. If you don't know what the problem is, you can't fix it.

Understanding as granular as possible is critical to knowing what that target needs at the time they need it."

BEING WHERE YOUR TARGET AUDIENCE CONGREGATES

One of the complaints I often hear from new business owners is how much time it takes to devote to social media. They have a presence on the majority of the platforms even if they're not maintained. Someone told them they needed to be on Snapchat so they opened an account. They didn't consider if their customer was there en mass or not. It was a social media channel and they needed to be there.

Well, million-dollar brands know that they only need to spend resources where their customers and potential clients congregate. That could be LinkedIn or Instagram.

The key is to learn where they show up and set up shop there. Kimmi Wernli of Crazy Richard's Peanut Butter shared what works for her million-dollar business.

> *"It comes down to one thing in the beginning. It is knowing your audience because the whole point in spending time or money or resources on a marketing platform is a waste if your target audience and end consumer is not there. If your end consumer is looking at traditional print media, then great. Buy print media!*
>
> *If your end consumer is only on social media platforms, then that's where you need to be. It's figuring out exactly who that end consumer is and then making sure that you are all over their platform, their preferred method of receiving information.*
>
> *We have a food product and our consumers are either in grocery stores or buying online and we're discovering that online grocery is becoming even larger.*

In the past, we've spent a lot of money on in-store marketing promotions like coupons, in-store signage or promotions on the shelf. Now, it's transitioning to online app usage. Grocery stores now have their apps with digital coupons, and other items to download.

Things are shifting. I've spent a lot of time figuring out who our consumers are, where they are getting their information and then making sure we all over that platform. We want to be in their line of sight."

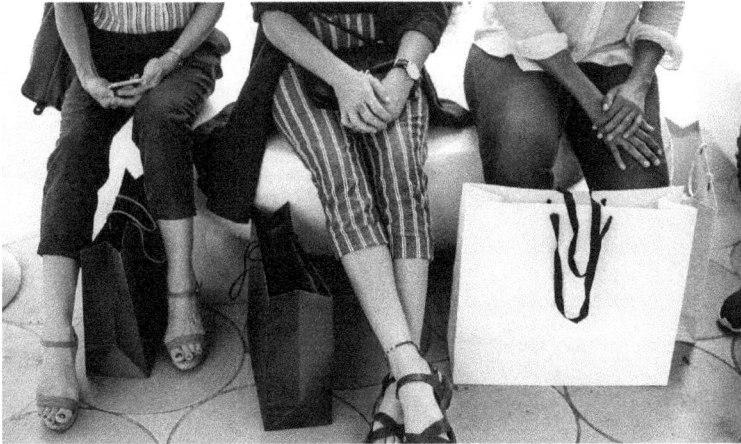

Customers

On shifting target audiences…

"Our customer base is a little difficult because we have such a wide consumer base. We consider

ourselves a family company. Our products appeal to consumers with dogs and infants up to a grandparent struggling with a heart condition or diabetes.

We have such a wide range of consumers, but the majority of those making purchases are women between the ages 25 to 45. So, we are trying to target the buyer. It's the soccer mom buyer that a lot of companies target because they are the largest spending group in the world.

I believe we appeal to everybody but has our consumer base phased out? Yes, to some extent. We now have millennials, Gen Z, and Gen X purchasing our products, but the most spending power is coming from women ages 25-45. We're trying to make sure we're figuring out how to connect with that consumer. We decided to hone in on exactly who this consumer is and gave them a face and a name; we call her Katie. So, we're constantly asking, "Is Katie is shopping at this store? Is Katie going to walk down this aisle? Is Katie going to open this app on her phone? How is she getting her information? How is she sharing that?"

This approach has helped us in making sure that from a marketing standpoint when we're spending money on time or talent, that it's something that will reach our consumer."

MILLION-DOLLAR QUESTIONS

- Have you defined your target audience?

- How would you have handled a 4 PM Money Meeting with a disgruntled key player?

- What are your target audience's pain points?

- What is your solution?

- How often are you probing for issues your target audience may be having?

- Are you actively refining your product or service?

- Are you creating new products or service to address new pain points?

CHAPTER FIVE

Traditional vs. Digital Marketing: The Many Ways to Market Your Business

*"I originally thought, "*Oh, maybe we can do this on a shoestring budget*" and we quickly realized that it costs to play in the digital arena."*

-Kimmi Wernli, Crazy Richard's Peanut Butter

"Marketing can be done a shoestring budget as long as you know exactly who your client is, who you are and what you're doing."

-Nancy Klensch, Summit Kids

More than a decade ago, experts said that digital would be the death of print media. The ease of posting newsletters, magazines, reports, case studies, even books online would do away with the need for printed material.

I don't know about you, but I still get direct marketing pieces in my mailbox, and can still buy printed versions of books, magazines, and newspapers. While the industry may not be as robust as it once was, its death isn't anytime soon.

So, when new business owners and entrepreneurs ask about marketing their businesses, they tend to only hear about digital marketing such as ads on social media and Google AdWords. This can leave many new business owners confused and over their marketing budgets.

A mentor once shared a story about a company who at the time did not have a social media presence. They had a website but had no LinkedIn profile, no Facebook page and certainly no Instagram account.

At the time, I was spewing out the latest facts from those in my industry who said you had to have a presence to make money. My mentor calmly explained that his client had no such presence but could send out a single email and generate tens of thousands of dollars in hours.

Still, some individuals only use social media platforms such as Instagram to sell product and are quite successful. Not to mention some still manage to generate healthy revenues on YouTube. These examples serve as a reminder that marketing isn't one-size-fits all.

Klensch of Summit Kids said this, "Know your target audience. Marketing could be endless, and you could throw billions at marketing if you're trying to market to everyone."

The bottom line for any company is to know your target audience, know where they congregate and set up camp there. And depending on your industry, that's going to look different from business to business.

Wernli of Crazy Richard's Peanut Butter stated earlier that it only makes sense to be on platforms where your target audience congregates. Sometimes that's print media, sometimes that on social media platforms like Snapchat. The link to how you market and where you show up online is tightly connected to knowing your target audience. Knowing this influences how and where you spend your marketing dollars.

VIDEO MARKETING

If you've ever had to take the seat cover off a car seat to wash it or reassemble a mobile playpen, you know how difficult those tasks can be. By the time you're ready for the first wash or set up the playpen at grandmas, the manual is long gone! And you need to get the cover back on quick because you have to go and pick up the other kids from school. So, where do most turn? When people want to know something, they go to YouTube.

The current metrics and ROI for video are undeniable. Video is yielding high customer engagement by the way of likes, shares, and comments. Even still, I hear it all the time from clients and business owners...I hate the way I look/sound on video! And because of this, they shy away from the platform when video is currently proving the most effective way of connecting in online spaces.

I also get asked, "Why go through the hassle of producing the video or go through the expense of having someone do it for you?" It all seems like a big hassle, right? It's easier to write an article or send a brochure.

Well, a marketing company called Wyzowl surveyed video usage and compiled a report based on their findings. They listed 30 facts from the study and here are my top three favorite reasons.

1. 79% of consumers would rather watch a video to learn about a product, than reading text on a page.

2. 98% of users say they've watched an explainer video to learn more about a product or service.

3. Video in an email leads to a 200-300% increase in click-through rates.

There's no arguing with the data. Video is a tool many brand owners are successfully using, even million-dollar ones and seeing outstanding results. Especially when you consider that:

- Online videos will account for more than 80% of all consumer Internet traffic by 2020.

- Social video generates 12 times more shares than text and images combined.

- Videos up to two minutes long get the most engagement.

- Native videos on Facebook have 10 times higher reach compared to YouTube links.

- People (i.e. your target audience) simply prefer video over text! Forbes reported that 59 percent of executives said they would rather watch a video than reading text.

- Forrester Research reported that it is 50x easier to achieve a page 1 ranking on Google with a video.

Facebook, Instagram, and even LinkedIn offer brand owners and marketing content creators the opportunity to produce live video directly from mobile or desktop devices.

Need any more convincing?

I reviewed two email campaigns I sent out for myself and noticed one of the video statistics was painfully accurate. I sent out two emails to two different audiences. I used a still image in one and a video in the other.

Here are my stats:

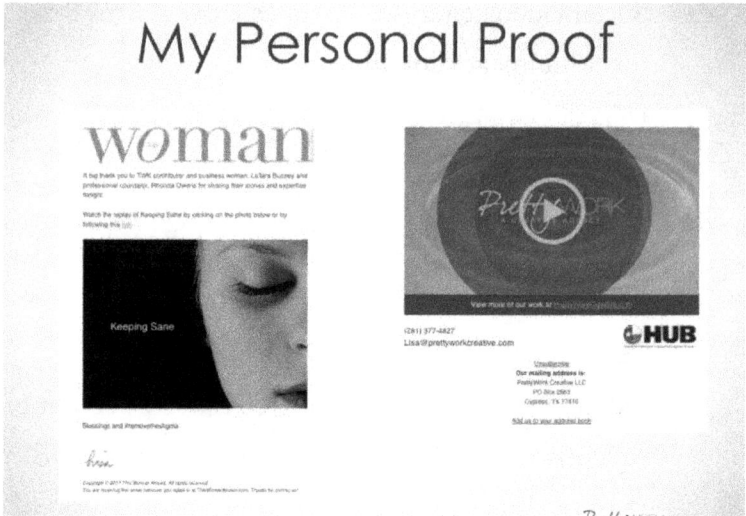

Two campaigns I sent out to two different audiences.

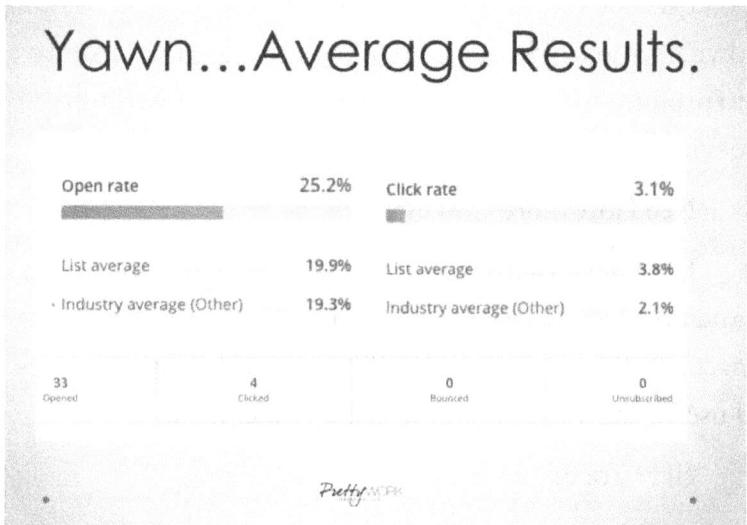

Open and click-through rates for an email with a photo.

50% Open Rate! Whoa!

Open rate		50.6%	Click rate		21.8%
List average		48.1%	List average		20.5%
Industry average (Other)		19.3%	Industry average (Other)		2.1%

79	34	4	1
Opened	Clicked	Bounced	Unsubscribed

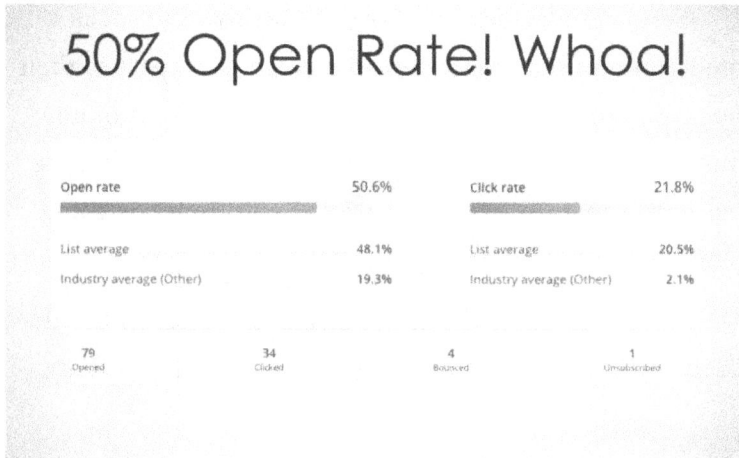

Open and click-through rates for an email with a video.

I didn't see the full 200% click-through rates the report mentioned but I did see a 157% increase, so I had no complaints! I'm convinced that video in email is an absolute win. That and using a subject line that gets people to open your email in the first place.

SOCIAL MEDIA

They probably won't admit it now, but many experts believed social media was a fad. They didn't think the platform was sustainable. But here we all are, feeling a little lost whenever Facebook or Instagram experiences an outage.

Social media has become for many brands, a vital tool when it comes to customer engagement, lead generation, and brand awareness.

Certain industries like hospitality now find social media and online review sites to be a critical part of their business. These tools are many times the geneses of new business. A review on Yelp could be mean the difference between someone booking a stay at your hotel or going elsewhere.

Jennifer Breen of SuiteHome says she and her team check all the major social media platforms almost daily.

> *"There are many choices when you're staying in any kind of rental accommodation, especially in Chicago. There are so many options. I honestly don't even know how many hotels and corporate housing options exist.*
>
> *So, for us, the strength of our brand is not only in having a ton of online reviews and a huge social media presence but to be visible on several platforms consistently. We're on LinkedIn, Facebook, Twitter, Instagram almost every single day.*
>
> *People want to see digital photos, so we give them digital photos. People want to see virtual tours, so now we offer virtual tours. We contracted and bought the same equipment that real estate brokerage firms use to showcase our apartments. Potential renters can walk into any of our apartments without physically being there.*

Branding is no longer what you say about your brand. It's a culmination of things and reviews play a big part in your brand message. With everything being virtual and online, potential guest asks, "Am I going to show up and the place look like what I see online?"

And I've had that happen to me before. I rented an apartment through www.vacationrentalbyowner. com in Colorado once and when I showed up, it was nothing like the pictures I saw.

For us, our brand is building upon our authenticity and providing a ton of support to show our customers that what they see online is what they'll get. It's hugely important in my industry. I mean, this will be a person's home away from home. They could be living there for a month or years. They want to know where they're getting.

We have to be authentic online. We had to adapt and allow people to see our apartments just as easily on their mobile phone as they could on their desktop and be able to reach us immediately through either social media platform.

We receive and respond to online messages all the time through Facebook and our website. For us, being present and active on social media is most important."

FACE-TO-FACE SELLING, RELATIONSHIP BUILDING

"I realized when it comes to marketing, we do what I call old-fashioned marketing. It's very much one on one and it has been invaluable in my business. It's all about relationships. Some people want to hear what you sound like and get a feel for you. They want to know if we have chemistry or not."

-Laura Yamanaka, TeamCFO

Million-dollar brands know that you can start a relationship online but to seal the deal, sometimes you have to do that offline in a face-to-face encounter.

Many of the service-based industries I spoke with, including engineering firms and consultants, did their marketing what's deemed the old-fashioned way: face-to-face. They attended trade shows and conferences. They went to highly niched events and marketed directly to the customer through the time-honored tradition of relationship building. The adage is still true, people do business with people they know, like and trust. This is especially true when you're talking B2B or high-dollar transactions and Vicki LaRose of Civil Design, Inc. agrees.

"The most successful business strategy that we've had is in attending conferences. Potential clients

attend these events and are typically more relaxed. I don't know about other markets but most of our client acquisition is relationship driven. By attending conferences, it's the only time you have access to them, and their guard is usually down as opposed to if we had scheduled a formal meeting. We take them to lunch because, everyone is more relaxed, and the client gets to know you better."

Nancy Klensch of Summit Kids also believes in the personal connection and has devised a method that strongly encourages customers to pick up the phone and call her center.

"We try not to eliminate the human connection from our marketing. We encourage contact with potential customers. And I think that's important because when it comes to marketing, it's "Check us out online" and "Click here to register and enter your credit card number." Now, we can do everything without ever interacting with another human being. I believe it is important for us to make sure that we still have that human connection. It's especially important since we're dealing with children. We encourage contact.

For instance, our marketing strategy dictates that we don't put any of our pricing information online.

So, we'll get a phone call and a parent will ask, "Well, how much are you? I don't see any prices online." And that's on purpose because now you called me.

Now, I can have a conversation and make a human connection and build trust. We get all the sexy marketing tips and tricks suggesting everything is electronic and automated, and these tools do everything for you. But when I built my company, I thought no; we want to talk to moms. We want to have that connection, and as women, connection is important. Parents want to look into the eyes of the person that's going to be raising their child because quite honestly, we're co-parenting. That's what childcare boils down to."

NETWORKING, TEACHING AND RELATIONSHIP BUILDING

One of the first things new entrepreneurs are encouraged to do is to start networking and meeting new people. If you've ever ventured to a meeting by yourself, you know how stressful networking events can be. Especially for introverted business owners. And there's always that one business owner who passes out cards to everyone, does all the talking and never engages in a real conversation. In a rapid-fire manner, they bombard you with who they are and what they do and while you're halfway through your business name, they're off to the next person.

But connecting with the right group can truly be beneficial to your business growth. Kristi Mirambell of K-Belle Consultants doesn't oppose networking but says it's not how she prefers to meet new people.

> *"The whole networking thing doesn't work for my personality. It's overly commercialized and seems like speed dating. You go talk about whatever you're supposed to talk about, and then you do the generic let's keep in touch and move on. It doesn't work for me.*
>
> *I teach classes at the Urban League and believe they sincerely care about small businesses. They hold members accountable.*
>
> *I appreciate more intimate settings. I'm outgoing, however, I enjoy settings where I can sit and have an authentic conversation. I don't want to sit there and pull out a PowerPoint presentation and tell you how good I am. I want to be real and honest. I want to share battle wounds; I want you to share battle wounds with me. I want to know that we're not here selling to each other. In my classes, we have a raw, authentic conversation because everyone's got*

a story, and everyone can bring something to the table. I prefer to build relationships that way.

For example, one evening I received a phone call at 5:30 from a man I'd never met. He says, "Hey Christi, you know so-and-so suggested I give you a call because they thought you could probably help me find an office. I wanted to start my business a year ago and am just now trying to get my feet off the ground. Can I meet with you and figure out how I can get an office this weekend?" I pondered how I could help this guy and decided to give him a call. I thought, he owns a trucking company and we use trucks; we do concrete work. So, I thought why not give him a chance. He's in business and he's humbled enough to ask for help. I just believe that the sharing economy comes full circle when it comes to building relationships."

JOINING ORGANIZATIONS

If you happen to live in a large city, business owners can typically find a host of organizations to join. Everything from chambers of commerce to networking groups to specialized business groups for the LGBTQ community or female contractors. These organizations exist to facilitate connections between other like-minded business owners who could potentially refer or do business with you.

Jennifer Breen of SuiteHome says that being an active member in a variety of organizations helps keep her brand in front of potential clients in a cost-effective way.

> *"We joined so many associations. I cannot even tell you how many. You have to remember that you are your brand when you are out and networking. We're part of every relocation council, every human resource council, every diversity council, and women's business council. We volunteer. We set up booths. We go to networking events. We make sure we are out there representing SuiteHome. Part of your brand is making sure people know who the company is, who you are, and do so without spending a bazillion dollars on national advertising."*

BILLBOARDS, WEBSITES, PRINT AND RADIO ADS

I attended a marketing event sponsored by our local daily paper. Because of digital's explosion, they have been able to fine-tune their demographics. They know exactly who's reading their printed paper. My representative told me that mature, affluent audiences subscribe and read their physical papers. She also said that there was an increase in print ads with the new postal rate increase.

It's cheaper to buy print ads than send out a direct mail campaign!

Loreen Gilbert of WealthWise Financial knows that her target audience reads influential publications such as local business journals and *The Wall Street Journal*. Advertising with business journals works for WealthWise because they, "do business with corporations and high net worth individuals" and those are the people who are reading business journals.

Klensch of Summit Kids said, "We don't do a lot of print marketing. I just don't find the return on it." She repeated the sentiment that you have to know what works for your business.

One dark day in 2019, Facebook and Instagram went down for hours and it was a reminder to business owners to have a presence outside of social media. Early on, it was heavily emphasized that being on social media was good, but you needed a home-base—your company's website. And then you also needed a strong email list for this very reason—social media sites go down, go away like Vine or become unpopular like Myspace.

LaRose recalled a moment when her building signage inspired a customer to find her online. She said:

> *"We had one client that said he drove by our building a billion times and then he went to our website and made a cold call. That never happens!*

Then he says, "I just want to meet you guys." Now, we are their trusted engineers. I never thought our website was that big of a deal, but people go there. Marketing is more than your brochure or what you hand out. It can also be your sign on the building that leads people back to your website."

LaRose also advises business owners to spend money on their websites and to make sure it tells the same story. LaRose continues, "Even in our business where social media isn't quite popular, people still go to our website to find out more."

WORD-OF-MOUTH AND REVIEW SITES

The Power of Word-of-Mouth Marketing
"We found that word of mouth works. I think when it comes to children, it's word of mouth—parent referrals. We harness the power of women creating that network around their children."

-Nancy Klensch, Summit Kids

I saw it for myself live and in real-time, the power of Word of Mouth Marketing or WOMM.

I was getting a pedicure at my favorite spa. I love this place for the atmosphere. No TVs blaring. Instead, Zen-like music plays and peace and tranquility ooze from the paint on the walls. It's typically quiet and patrons understand it's a moment to unwind.

Two fellow patrons, also getting pedicures appeared to be hungry, based on their conversation. One of them wanted a Philly-style cheesesteak; it was quite serious for her. She Googled the closest restaurant to serve such, told her friend that as soon as her toenail polish dried, she was on her way to satisfy her craving for this cheesy, beefy concoction.

That's when it happened.

A woman not originally part of this conversation came out of her pedicure-induced meditative state and said, "Oh no, you don't want to eat there. I work across the street from that place and it's horrible."

And just like that, it was done.

This business lost a customer just like that and maybe even more since we were all forced into this conversation.

This business wasn't even given the chance and lost out on what could have been a loyal customer all because of one woman's testimonial.

Who knows the CLV (customer lifetime value) this business lost due to word of mouth marketing?

Customer service—not clever slogans—is what can make or break a company.

THE NUMBERS ON WOMM

When word of mouth is positive, it is a company's

best friend. In my nail shop scenario, it was the kiss of death. In addition to having a good product, customer service must always be on point; without fail. And on the sad occasion where there is a breakdown, a company must make it right and let its customers know it's been addressed and resolved. I don't know if the woman who shot down the cheesesteak business had visited this place many times since it was close to her job or if patrons that worked in her office complained regularly. Whatever the case, there's an issue the franchise owner is either unaware of or not willing to fix. Either it way it cost him. No slick commercial, direct-mail campaign or two-for-one coupon can help if no change to service is being made.

- It's no surprise that 84% of consumers say they either "completely or somewhat trust recommendations from family and friends about products." That makes recommendations from this information source the highest-ranked for trustworthiness. The women at the nail shop were strangers but the shared pedicure experience was enough to dissuade one woman from even trying the restaurant.

- This WOMM doesn't just impact business-to-consumer companies either. B2B companies can benefit or not benefit from WOMM too. Ninety-one percent of B2B buyers reported that they are influenced by WOM when making their decision to buy.

- This last stat is what was proved right in front of me that day in the nail shop; 84% of consumers reported always or sometimes taking action based on personal recommendations. Seventy percent said they did the same based on online consumer opinions.

HOW TO LEVERAGE WORD-OF-MOUTH (WOM)

According to RetaileWire, Millennials and Baby Boomers ranked WOM as the number one marketing influencer in certain purchasing decisions and for other items, WOM ranked as high as third. So how can a business take advantage or seed WOM among customers?

Creating exceptional customer experiences should be the norm, not the exception.

People tend to share when there's something in it for them, like additional discounts, great swag or free items or gift cards. In a survey conducted by Software Advice, more than 50% of survey respondents said they were likely to give a referral if offered a direct incentive, social recognition or access to an exclusive loyalty program.

Even social recognition is a valuable commodity. Sixty-six percent of respondents under the age of 35 said they were more likely to give a referral after receiving social recognition.

People do talk about your business. What they say depends on the quality of your product, the customer service you offer and what cool thing you're giving away...whether it be social recognition, gift cards or cool swag.

You want to make sure that when a bunch of women gets together to collectively soak their toes, should your company come up...they'll have good things to say.

WHEN WOM MOVES ONLINE - ONLINE REVIEWS

With the birth of social media came a lot of trepidation from businesses of all sizes. For all the opportunities to engage with the customer and learn their needs, fear paralyzed many.

I remember sitting in a meeting with a marketing director and VP of Sales where they discussed their fear of traversing into online spaces. They were afraid of receiving negative reviews. Rather than reap the benefits of online customer engagement by putting into place people, procedures and policies to handle all reviews, they opted out which is a shame.

Million-dollar brand owners know that conversations

about their business happens on and offline whether they like it or not. So, it's best to be in a place where you can respond, learn and possibly win over a customer.

Million-dollar brand owner Limaris Alvarado of Echo Consulting said this about the WOMM surrounding her business:

> *"We didn't have a formal sales force in place to credit our company growth. Instead, our growth happened because of word-of-mouth. We were mainly focused on providing excellent service. I'm proud to say that marketing happens when you provide excellent service."*

MANAGING REVIEWS

With the growth of eCommerce and social media came online reviews. Site's like Yelp, Amazon and Angie's List allow customers to share their customer experience, good or bad. Million-dollar brands recognize this and allocate resources to respond to reviews. Marcelle Flower of Armstrong Plumbing shares her experience.

> *"We live in a time when review sites like Yelp and Angie's List are extremely popular. Even with all these different resources that highlight the good, it still means something when a neighbor says, "Call these guys," or a family member says, "They*

were just at my home and I've never had such a great experience."

We make sure that the customer's experience is one hundred percent satisfactory and if it's not, then we owe the customer that experience. My biggest source of growth has been from customer retention and being able to turn things around on these types of review sites.

So, what happens on the off chance you get a bad review? It does happen and you have to know how you'll handle an immature response. You have to know you can't please everyone. Someone is going to have a bad day or have a preconceived idea about the service they were to receive, or some people are just wired wrong! You won't be able to change everyone's perception.

If an issue is brought to our attention, we address it immediately and not even seconds later, we'll see a good online review."

Merrilee Kick of Southern Champion understands that customer queries can come through social media channels as well as the company's website. She suggests the following:

"A lot of times, you'll get a question on social media and your website. Make sure everybody has a way to communicate back to the customer. Have an email address where they can email you and ask you questions. If you don't respond promptly, you lose the customer. I've found that I can get customers for life just by responding to either somebody's complaint or their question. I'm the president of the company and I respond to their question. They're going, 'oh my god, I never thought I'd hear from the president of the company. This is amazing!" It makes them feel good.

I check social media every day. I'm not the only one to respond. Thankfully, I have a team of people in marketing that respond to customers as well. We're quick to send swag to people if somebody complains about something. Maybe all they wanted is a fanny pack or something like that and then they're happy. Then they're promoting and doing other stuff so they can get more stuff."

Kimmi Wernli of Crazy Richard's Peanut Butter offered these sage words of advice when it comes to marketing:

"When people ask me questions about marketing, I tell them it's about figuring out your target

consumer and then making sure you're showing up all over their preferred platform. Whether it is traditional print, in-store, out-of-store, word-of-mouth, whatever it is, that is how you're attacking your consumer, making sure that you're getting your brand in front of that consumer. It's different for every business, and every owner has to identify its consumer.

Have we spent a lot of money on marketing? In the past, we didn't. We did not spend money on print media or digital marketing, and it was mostly the money that we would spend in a store. But now, like you, I thought, "Oh, maybe we can do this on a shoestring budget," and we very quickly realized that it costs to pay to play in the digital arena.

If you want to be involved and get your product out there, digitally you have to be strategic or else you are going to spend a lot of money and some companies are far larger than mine that have plenty of money to put towards digital marketing.

So, I make sure that every dollar that we're putting towards marketing is not just money that we're throwing away. It's money that's being used strategically."

KEEP MARKETING EVEN
AFTER THE BIG CLIENT WIN

No matter which methodology you use to market your business, million-dollar brand owner, Jill Kerrigan of JAK Design said, "Never stop marketing your business."

New business development is a critical component of your business growth. Kerrigan confessed that she put all of her eggs in one *American Express* basket and when that client didn't renew their contract, she had to restart all of her marketing efforts. She said she had to restart her marketing a second time when two out of the three big clients she had also didn't renew.

Kerrigan says, "you have to diversify" and "never stop marketing yourself even when you're at your busiest."

"The last thing entrepreneurs do is put their marketing needs first which is something I had not done in my own business. It makes a huge difference. It was hard to get my employees to understand that it's easy to get a big client and keep the big client but when you have three different huge business units with one client and the two business units drop their projects, well then, you're in trouble.

You have got to diversify. Client diversification is the most important thing. I started by putting all my eggs in the one American Express basket. It was back in the day—23 years ago when there was money aplenty.

But then, 2008 hit and then, 2013 hit and I had just laid off four people because American Express dropped two of their big programs that we ran. I decided to start a new business to help acquire new business to sustain us while I worked on growing my primary business."

MILLION-DOLLAR QUESTIONS

- What marketing methodologies are you using in your business (social media, personal selling, direct mail)?

- Are these methodologies working for your business?

- Do you set goals you can measure for your various marketing campaigns?

- How are you managing online reviews?

- Are there any methodologies you want to look into as a way to expand your reach and increase revenue?

CHAPTER SIX

Employees Are Brand Ambassadors: Hire the Right People

"We have an external client and an internal client. And we have to make sure that our internal client— meaning our staff—is also educated; that they're kept in the loop. We tell them about the exciting things that are going on and keep them encouraged."

-Nancy Klensch, Summit Kids

Million-dollar brands understand that their greatest resource is the human one, their employees. Fail here and your brand doesn't stand a chance no matter how good your marketing and social media campaigns are.

Zappos founder, Tony Hsieh understood this and built the company on the premise that employees come first. They come before shareholders, stakeholders, vendors, suppliers and even the customer.

Why?

Because these are the people on the front lines of your business. These are the people customers are interacting with and this interaction can make or break your bottom line. Your employees are the face of your brand, therefore, having the right people in the right place is paramount.

Get this wrong and recovering your brand's good name could be long and arduous.

According to a Forbes article by Blake Morgan, "Customer service is a $750 billion-dollar industry." Companies are spending billions on employee training, team-building exercises and new technologies all to keep employees happy and happily serving the people who pay the bills—the customer.

THE COST OF HIRING THE WRONG PEOPLE

I met Catherine at a women's networking meeting. She's dedicated to influencing change in the lives of people living with disabilities and marginalized youth through her nonprofit organization. As we went around the room and introduced ourselves, we were instructed to share one thing we were currently looking for help within our business. Catherine briefly mentioned that her marketing new hire wasn't working out and she was looking for a solution.

After the meeting, we chatted, and she shared that

she had been responsible for all the marketing work. She and her business partner were relieved when they thought they found someone to shoulder that responsibility. This new hire was supposed to free her and her business partner up to focus on the bigger aspects of their business-like fundraising and expansion.

Except it didn't work out that way. Instead, Catherine found herself having to redo work she had assigned the new hire. Even after thoroughly explaining the project and outlining the expectations, the new hire failed to deliver. The business partner even questioned their ability to communicate. They didn't understand why their new hire could not or would not deliver the work they asked for. They were once again looking to solve a problem they thought they had already solved.

An Employer's Worst Nightmare

Of all the interviews I conducted for this book, it was Biddie Webb's story of LIMB Design that kept my mouth agape during the entire interview. Webb is a partner at her sister's firm, and she describes in detail the malicious behavior by an employee they treated like family.

> *"In growing the business, there have been many times that we felt we had the right person in the right place only to find out that we had it all wrong. We had a situation where we hired an*

employee that was not only talented but had the vision to take the firm to the next level in both reputation and introducing new offerings. We felt this person would be a great fit for a partnership which was a very serious and expensive decision for us. We believed in this person, did everything we could both financially and emotionally to show how much we appreciated the work, vision, goals, growth, and reputation that had been put forth and, as a result offered them a partnership.

We then offered this individual a partnership only to find out that it was not a true and transparent relationship. Literally in one day, our company changed when this person had been planning and executing a new company months before—strategically planning to destroy our firm as they start theirs. It's not unusual for entrepreneurial people to leave and go after their dreams. We embrace this trait. However, it was done so maliciously it should have destroyed our firm. They took our top, lucrative clients, deleted files from the server, sent notices to our clients that we were discontinuing our core business offering. It took weeks and months to recover. With the help of great friends and clients that were loyal to Limb in past years, we reinvented ourselves and became stronger and more focused despite this unfortunate chapter in our three decades of being in business.

Presently, what we have learned is that when hiring for positions, we don't look at how things are at that moment, but how things would be if it unraveled. We found out that nothing stays constant—change always happens—including people. It's how one becomes resilient to change and can adjust and refocus on what is ahead of them—not what is behind them that makes them survive. It has also taught us to recognize the 'signs' when employees or management begin to 'go dark.' Are they distant, non-communicative, defensive, argumentative? When people have secrets, their personality changes and when employees or management begins to change or become distant or 'dark', our radar tells us what is about or could occur. We have not been wrong in our hunches since then.

This experience has also forever changed how we hire and vet people to work with us. Now, we're not necessarily looking for the best and brightest. Not to say that our team isn't talented because they are, and we still make them a part of our Limb family.

But we look for other traits such as character and personality and if that person fits within our culture. We can always train people. Character matters most for us."

HIRING THE RIGHT PEOPLE

Business speaker and blogger, Jay Goltz wrote a piece for The New York Times and confirms what every business owner knows: you cannot build a company without the right people. Hiring the right people, according to Goltz, "Requires both a great hiring protocol and the stomach to make the changes that become necessary as the company grows. Especially when it turns out that people who were 'right' at the beginning are no longer 'right' in their roles as the company grows."

Assess Your Needs

Sometimes you need a direct hire. Other times a temporary employee. In other instances, you may need to hire a consultant. The latter was true for one small business.

It had been months since the business had posted anything to their blog and they were out of ideas on how to generate new leads. Their solution was to recruit a low-level marketing employee who would divide their time between blog writing and creating lead generating strategies. Months later, they found themselves with new blog posts but no clear strategy on gaining new prospects into their sales funnel and they were frustrated.

Two Possible Solutions

One solution would have been to hire a marketing consultant. Someone who could create and implement a marketing strategy on the company's behalf.

Another option would have been to restructure the department and hire a marketing executive who could create such strategies and have the low-level marketing hire implement the program.

Instead, they found themselves with no real solution to move the organization forward.

Hire Slow, Fire Fast

In 2014, I had the opportunity to interview Arquella Hargrove, an HR expert on my podcast show, ShopTalk with The Marketing Stylist™. In that interview, she said something I have always remembered, "hire slow, fire fast." Meaning take your time and find the right person. The main reason being cost. Hiring someone who isn't a good fit cost you time and money. Keeping someone ill-suited for the role assigned to them can cost you customers, money, morale, and productivity. So, the assumption that someone is better than no one isn't true. Especially if you're having to redo all the work or you're losing customers during the process.

Train the Right People

Even if your business doesn't have the budget to hire seasoned and experienced professionals, the rule is to then hire talent. Hire employees who show flexibility and who are teachable. Hire passionate people who embody the mission and values of your company. This is why Hargrove suggests a slow hiring process.

If the people who were 'right' at the beginning are no longer 'right' in their roles, you could consider:

- Reassigning them to another task or role within the company

- Offer training or education if there is interest and/or potential for growth

- Simply let them go, and remember to do so quickly

HIRING FAMILY AND THE 1099 EMPLOYEE

Most small business owners and clients I know have at some point hired friends and family to work in their business. Especially when you're just starting.

Many times, these are not the people that will have these roles long term but believe in your vision and want to help.

When hiring staff—whether it be family members or friends—many small business owners consider bringing on new hires as 1099 employees. The employee is treated as a contractor and is responsible for their payroll taxes. There are strict rules and guidelines on 1099 employees and not following them could cost your company greatly so it's worth it to do your research. Hire an attorney or HR expert if need be.

Flower of Armstrong Plumbing hired her son to work in the business initially as a mechanic. She said that he was a good mechanic but when the company needed a video, he stepped up to the challenge and produced a great video. Now he works in their marketing department.

Kick of Southern Champion admitted to paying family and friends pennies on the dollars!

> *"When I started the company, I didn't have any money to hire anybody. I hired my family and paid them pennies on the dollar to work for me. Sometimes, I paid with a beer! I just didn't have the money to hire people, so I ended up hiring our friends and many of my son's friends.*
>
> *It was mainly to work in the warehouse, cleaning things during the summer and wasn't long-term. Then, three years in, things started getting serious and we needed more people. It was time to start hiring more experienced people.*

So, it's important to think about the maturity level of the people you hire. You could hire somebody that has a great education, but maybe they don't have the right personality. Maybe they're too serious or they're just not a fun person. That can drive you crazy. In some cases, the personality of that person is more important than their education."

YOUR EMPLOYEES ARE THE FACE OF YOUR BRAND

During my interview with Nancy Klensch of Summit Kids, one thing was very clear, she sees her employees as the face of her brand and treats them as such.

"Every person we employ is a salesperson. Every employee is a marketing person. I have 100 people on my team, and I say we have 100 people on our marketing team because they are the face of the brand. What people experience when they come to our company and receive our service is the brand.

The brand is not what I say it is. The brand is not what my marketing says it is. It's what happens on our front line. It's what happens in those classrooms with those kids. That's our brand.

My view on marketing is that we have an external client and an internal client. And we need to make sure that our internal client, meaning our staff, is educated. We make sure that they're kept in the loop. We tell them all the exciting things going on. And we also encourage them to live the values we have in place. The value that says we're trying to teach these kids. I'm hiring true believers. They have to believe in what we're doing and why we're doing it and in our client. They represent us all the time, everywhere they go. When they're out at a barbecue for the weekend and somebody asks, "Who do you work for?" If we've done our job right and empowered our employee, they're positively marketing our brand at that moment.

Big mistakes come from companies that don't realize that every single person in their company is essentially their marketing team. I think that's the untapped marketing secret.

I think people look for the big, flashy new thing. I'm always asked, well what about Facebook ads or maybe you should be getting into this new thing or maybe you should blog or vlog. You know the list goes on and on with all the things you can do to get your name out there. But what we don't realize is the power of the people who are already here—our employees. We've already sold them.

They've come to us looking for employment and we've hired them; hopefully, it's a great match. We need to utilize them and make sure that they have the skills, confidence, and passion to carry that marketing message."

When Employees Challenge the Brand

As stated earlier, Klensch is passionate about face-to-face interactions when it comes to her customers. She values this experience so much, that when an encounter went wrong, what to do came easy for her. Her manager struggled with the decision but in the end, the brand was saved.

"We had an employee who wasn't very friendly with our parents and he ended up getting into an argument with one of the dads. He was great with the kids and everybody loved him but when it came to parent interaction, he was a bit of a jerk. So, I told one of my managers that we needed to remove him. He didn't represent what we valued. This was not the type of behavior we wanted on our team.

My manager at that time was very hesitant because it's hard to fire somebody. The manager thought that perhaps it was just a miscommunication issue between the employee and the dad. He insinuated that maybe it wasn't the employee's fault. That may be the dad was the one being a jerk. And I said to him, "Well, this customer took the time to write me an email to complain. And we're not going to split hairs on who's right or who's wrong." At the end of the day, the employee is not representing our brand.

This manager was still very hesitant and said he was not comfortable firing him over the issue. So, I said to our manager, "You either fire him or you go over there and you fire our marketing manager." You can imagine that caught him completely off guard. I explained that if that employee's behavior is reflective of our brand, if our customer experience is going to be negative on the front line, then we don't need a marketing manager. I don't need somebody to update our website and tweet and do all of those things when that experience is not in alignment with our values.

I said, "You know we only need one of them. So, if you love this guy and you think he needs to hang around, then you go and you fire her." I didn't let him do that. But he kind of just looked at me and was surprised. I reiterated to him, "I don't need her updating brochures. I don't need her trying to find the perfect words to describe us if parents are going to run into this employee."

OH, THE THINGS YOU'LL LEARN DURING AN INTERVIEW!

American poet and civil rights activist, Maya Angelou once said, "When people show you who they are, believe them." This should be every entrepreneur and hiring manager's motto! People do show us who they are, even during the interview process and it's up to us to believe them. Angelou also said, "Never get mad at someone for being who they've always been. Be upset with yourself for not coming to terms with it sooner." This is another reason to hire slow. Merrilee Kick of Southern Champion offers her own valid reasons to do so as well.

> *"During the interview process, sometimes it's good to ask why potential hires want to leave their current job or what are some of the worst-case scenarios that happened at that job. You will be surprised by the stuff people will say. They say:*

> - *"When I didn't get hired, I called the I.R.S. and turned them in."*
>
> - *"I filed a harassment claim against them because they were always after me."*

- *"I wanted time off to be with my baby and they never let me have time off so I would just fake and be sick."*

- *"When I got in trouble, there'd be an argument."*

It's a fair warning when you hear about all the things these people have done to previous employers. Don't take it lightly.

They don't realize they're being judged on how they would treat you as their new employer. It's interesting especially when you hear that they've been tracking their boss and trying to determine how to turn them in. It's all very telling."

MILLION-DOLLAR QUESTIONS

- Are there non-critical tasks that friends or family could help you with?

- Is a 1099 contract employee the right choice for your business?

- Are your company culture, mission, and values already in place?

- How will you handle HR duties such as payroll, policies, and benefits?

- How could a business protect itself against what happened to LIMB Design?

- Do you agree with Nancy Klensch of Summit Kids decision to fire the employee who didn't live up to the brand?

- Do you have a social media policy in place for employees?

CHAPTER SEVEN
Leveraging PR, Sponsorships, and Appointments

In addition to personal selling, digital marketing, social media and running print ads, PR also falls under the marketing umbrella. When done correctly, PR gets you seen by the right people, in the right places and positively impacts your company's bottom line.

You could do this yourself.

Technically you could.

But what million-dollar brands know is that it takes established relationships and connections to effectively launch a PR campaign.

If you're a small business owner, you've likely heard that you should follow the influencers, bloggers, writers, journalists on Twitter and other social media networks. Small businesses are encouraged to learn the patterns of these key media holders, applaud their work, offer up suggestions and leads (not your own at first) with the hopes of building a relationship and gaining their trust. Then, you pitch them with your idea or story.

According to Josh Sternberg's article in Entrepreneur. com, "Many small business owners send out pay upwards of $500 for a press release that's released to top-tier sources, normally to only sit on dedicated sites that host thousands of such releases. One such PR service company said they process 80,000 press releases a day."

And still, some small business owners, write their press releases and send them out to local and national media professionals with the hope of getting seen and that better yet that elusive unicorn, free publicity. And a few individuals unknowingly get themselves blacklisted because they don't follow protocol. Meaning they call frequently to ask the influencer if they received their email. They flood inboxes and voicemails with, "did you get it yet" messages and don't realize they'll never get called back.

Some small businesses do manage to get through and win the prized unicorn of TV coverage or a magazine or newspaper writeup. It could be because it was a slow news week, the business was unique and interesting, had a great local, community component or a combination of any of these.

Million-dollar brands know that hiring the right

PR firm, one that specializes in your industry, has connections to influencers in that industry and is worth every penny. A few of the business owners I interviewed said they know this is a line item in the budget that not every small business can afford. One million-dollar brand owner said she set her marketing budget as a percentage of her overall profit year-after-year. Some years she was able to dedicate more to marketing and PR efforts than others, but she had a budget and stuck with it.

Gilbert of WealthWise Financial said that she's very strategic with social media and PR because you could end up spending a lot of money if you're not strategic. She sets a goal for the year and then meets with the entire team so strategies can be integrated and help the business achieve its goals.

PR AS PART OF YOUR GROWTH STRATEGY

Gilbert wanted to grow her business and had a clear vision for that growth. She would do so through mergers and acquisitions and her PR partner would play a significant role in her company reaching that goal and that meant getting more exposure.

She said:

> *"My goal for my company is to move from a regional firm to a national firm and leverage social media and PR to accomplish that goal. I'm*

very well-known locally but not as well known nationally. My goal is to have my social media and PR team help me become that national figure I want to be in the wealth management world. I've built my practice organically to this point. To grow ten times more, it's going to take me acquiring practices. That's where marketing and PR can help because as I become more well known on a national scale, advisors who are looking to retire would then already know who I am."

A Regional or National Reach?

Kimmi Wernli of Crazy Richard's Peanut Butter has used both a regional and national PR agency for her business. In the end, the national reach is what worked best for her business but suggests a regional reach can do wonders for the right business.

"Another thing we started to pay for last year was PR and that's a little bit different from social media marketing. PR is more high level. It's business-to-business and our PR agency submits our name to different magazine outlets within our industry. Initially, we hired a local agency here in Columbus, Ohio but that didn't work for us because we are a national brand. We needed someone that had more of a national presence. We found a PR company

in New York City that has worked with a lot of smaller natural food companies just like ours and that has worked for us.

They know the food industry and we're involved with a lot of natural products publications. They already have the connections and know the right editors to pitch the stories and send the press releases when something happens, or a new product comes out.

Hiring the right PR firm will depend on your needs. The PR agency I know and love in Columbus, Ohio represented a friend, another NAWBO sister. She owns a chain of kids' swimming lesson places and they're doing a fantastic job. They're crushing it in because it's locally based.

It's about finding the right agencies and partners in the marketing or social media space that fit your size or your niche. For us, we needed to find someone that was the right size, the right price and in the right industry to help us get in front of the right people. It takes time and energy. Signing a year-long contract with somebody with the hopes of everything working out is a big commitment and quite scary."

REGIONAL REACH BEFORE NATIONAL

Some publicists and PR firms will advise you to strive for local or regional exposure before going national and there are lots of good reasons for doing so. Building support from your local community is always a good thing.

A documentary I helped produce went national before it went local and did so very unintentionally.

My husband Elgin and I followed a team of volunteers for six weeks after Hurricane Harvey pummeled the city of Houston and surrounding areas. It was reported on news stations across the country that Harvey dumped 27 trillion gallons of water or four feet of water over four days. Then there was the intentional release of the Addicks and Barker Reservoirs that flooded many homes and businesses.

Houston was underwater and the storm and its aftermath didn't discriminate. The wealthiest of our communities, as well as those living in the margins and everyone in between, were impacted.

Elgin and I took what we thought would be a promo video piece for an organization and turned it into a nearly 30-minute documentary called *What Mercy Looks Like*. The film showed the cleanup efforts through the eyes of volunteers who came from all across the country to help Houstonians get back on their feet.

Once the documentary was completed, I did what any other small business owner would do. I wrote a press release and submitted it to a few PR outlets and to a few local media contacts I had.

The Weather Channel was the first to pick up the story and Elgin and I conducted an on-air interview via Skype. We went national before we went local.

So if you are looking to build your brand through PR without the help of a publicist or PR firm, you have to be smart, be patient, tap those trusted relationships and be willing to put yourself out there.

Yes, you should build local community support but know when your story has a broader reach and don't be afraid to aim high.

LEVERAGING PR

Depending on your business, there are many ways you can leverage PR to grow your business, especially if you have multiple audiences. Kimmi Wernli of Crazy Richard's Peanut Butter uses PR to target members who read trade publications, take part in industry organizations and then to their end consumer.

Wernli also shares that she wasn't always in a place to invest in PR and contemplates how an earlier investment in PR might have influenced her business.

"We have several target audiences and connect

with them in different ways. There are natural product trade publications, we have memberships in organizations such as the American Peanut Council and then there's our consumer, the 'Katies' of the world. Our PR agency is constantly pitching our products and story headlines to the kind of publications where 'Katie' may be reading.

In addition to targeting 'Katie,' they're making connections with larger influencers, with companies or just publications in general that are writing digital media, print media and local media. They're reaching out to all of our audiences and allocate their time between them accordingly. At the end of the month, they put together a slide deck of all of the gained or earned media that we were placed in for the month.

We take that information to our buyers and brokers. We share it with our sales force who are going around selling our products and say, "Hey, look at all of the media outlets in your area where consumers are seeing our products," and that will help them be more inclined to continue to put our products on the shelf."

Investing in PR

"PR agencies have the right connections if you find

the right person that's servicing your industry. For our company, it was the right time to find a national PR company to help us grow our business. I'm not sure that I would have said that five years ago or when we were smaller. I don't know. Maybe we would have changed, maybe it would have increased our sales. That's hard to say.

It's a huge investment for a small startup company. When I compare our company to other products or companies that sell natural products in the same industry, ones that are similar in size and have the fast-paced growth, it is all marketing. They usually have a lot of seed money or they raise a lot of funding and most of that money goes towards marketing.

Nobody just walks around and buys a new product they've never heard of. It's less likely for you to move your product unless someone has recommended it or it comes with some kind of catchy marketing involved.

It's hard to say what would have happened if we hired a firm early on, but for us, this was a great time for us to invest in PR. I think there are other types of marketing that a startup or a smaller company can use that's more budget-friendly until they can afford to invest in PR."

DOING GOOD IN YOUR NEIGHBORHOOD

Community events and sponsorships also fall under public relations and there are opportunities to grow your brand in these spaces as well. Million-dollar brands know this and capitalize on such events. Participating in community events and sponsoring brand-worthy events is a way to build goodwill and gain positive exposure.

Flower laughingly said her business is only thought of in times of crisis, so her business is not always top of mind. She employs a different approach to staying top of mine. She does some radio advertising but also relies on reviews and word-of-mouth marketing. When I asked her what else works for her, she said being out in the community. Setting up small booths that only cost a couple of hundred dollars have been beneficial. Sponsoring the local baseball team are all low-budget options with big returns.

She also said:

> *"I'm in the community a lot and I had a friend one time tell me the best source of advertising is just being out there. That was wise counsel. If there is a large women's gathering or women's group or a nonprofit doing something in the community, I*

like to be there and just get my face recognized. And it's working.

Recently, we had a women's night out with one of the local charities. There were probably 1,500 women there and I asked if I could have a minute or two on stage. I wanted to show women how to get their garbage disposal unplugged because sometimes they put potato peels into the disposal. They didn't know there was a little switch on the bottom of the garbage disposal. We give away the little wrenches and show them how to find the switch and get the garbage disposal started again. I tell women how to freshen their garbage disposal with lemon rinds and ice cubes.

Those kinds of things stick because it shows I want to help. I also educate women on how to locate their water valve so they can turn it off in case of an emergency."

According to Flower, this strategy works. It follows the *give something valuable away for free* marketing strategy small businesses hear so much about.

What I love is that she does so in person, so her target audience sees her, hears her voice, sees her warmth and compassion and willingness to help and that helps establish trust. Because the adage is true, people do business with people they know, like and trust.

SPONSORSHIP AND SWAG

Million-dollar brands know that sponsoring or partnering with the right event can be a huge win or it could be an epic fail. Sponsoring events isn't a new strategy and it's still effective. A colleague and dear friend sponsored a women's roller derby team and was pleased with her ROI. Her logo was everywhere! In the rink, on the program, on their website...whenever you saw the team, you saw her business. The partnership resulted in greater exposure of her brand and increased attendance at her events.

When you sponsor an event (or decide to vend at an event) the right swag is everything. The right giveaway or promo item will hopefully survive the event and make it back home with your target audience member.

It pays to be thoughtful about your swag and if you have the budget, be creative and stay true to your brand's personality.

Merrilee Kick of Southern Champion understands the power of swag and shares her story.

> *"We recently did a promo event at Jackson Hole and our tent was branded with our slogan BuzzBallz... Have a Ball! in bright red colors with white text.*

Under the tent, we hand out fun swag and do tastings.

During spring break with college kids, we hand out condoms with the BuzzBallz brand. They say, "Wrap it before you tap it!" and funny things like that. This has nothing to do with our brand other than the fact that it's fun and makes people laugh.

We have cell phone backers and bandannas and things that center around having fun. Our cell phone backers are popular because when ladies go out to party, they don't want to carry a purse. So, they use our cell phone backer to secure their credit cards and I.D. Our swag centers around fun.

We promoted our masculine brand, Crooked Fox Bourbon at a PBR (Professional Bull Riders) event. It speaks to feminine bourbon drinkers too. We gave out straw cowboy hats that were branded with the Crooked Fox Bourbon logo. Ironically, there was a vendor right around the corner from us trying to sell 200 or so hats. Many of which were straw hats and here we were giving them away. The entire rodeo was wearing our branded straw hats. That's the power of swag!"

LEVERAGING APPOINTMENTS, AWARDS, AND HIGH-PROFILE INTERVIEWS

As a business owner, you might find yourself being offered appointments to a city task force or a board seat. These appointments can give you and your brand increased exposure and new connections. So, do these appointments always translate into increased business or add to a brand's bottom line? Depends on who you ask.

Laura Yamanaka of TeamCFO said this regarding her SEC appointment:

> *"If the question is, did someone ever say to me, "I see you were appointed to the SEC ACSEC committee, so can I give you this opportunity?", the answer is no. I do think occasionally when people learned of my experience, it allowed them to view me in a different perspective both good and not so helpful. I thought it would always be a benefit! Upon reflection, it reinforced the concept that all of your experiences can work for you and against you in any particular situation. You may or may not be allowed to capitalize or deflect the good or the bad. I learned not to worry but be prepared if the benefit or issue is brought up."*

Lisa Scott of Scott Global Migration Law Group has seen her business revenue grow fivefold due to a concerted effort to win international awards within her industry.

"When I was ready to scale my business, I strategically decided to go after prestigious awards and recognitions. I targeted those that would put our firm on the international map and went after them. These awards can't be bought and they're not part of any kind of advertising—you have to earn them. These awards require that clients and peers say good things about you and then your information is put into these nice booklets and lists. And then you find yourself to be one of the few certified women-owned businesses in the U.S. on that list. That helped me gain an international reputation.

During my research, I learned that I not only had to do good work, but I had to know other lawyers. So, I joined chat groups, and conference groups, and instead of saying no, I said yes to speaking opportunities in Dubai and Amsterdam. Again, I was very strategic in pursuing international opportunities so that I could get my name out there. So, when this list of lawyers goes out, I'm on the list.

Crooked Fox Swag! Straw Cowboy Hats at Montana PBR.
Courtesy of Merrilee Kick

Because in the past, I would go after opportunities and the reason I wasn't selected in some cases would be because I wasn't known internationally, or not enough lawyers knew about me. Although I was passed over for those opportunities, I strategically went about changing that.

My annual gross income has gone up fivefold since 2015. We went from $300K to $1.5 million in gross revenue because companies now see us. Let me be honest, I'm a female lawyer running a business in a male-dominated space. I've had clients call me and ask me if I could do this work. The answer was always, of course, we could. But I sincerely believe that this international recognition, receiving all these awards just like other big law firms has put me in the running for bigger opportunities. I just got an email from a Fortune 200 company that is getting ready to change their immigration attorney and asked me to submit my information. Those awards put me on the map and made room for me to get inquiries like this."

MILLION-DOLLAR QUESTIONS

- Do you have a compelling story to tell?

- Do you need local or national exposure?

- What local events or organizations can you support to show community goodwill and gain brand exposure?

- Besides pens and mugs, what other creative items could you give away as swag (promotional items)?

CHAPTER EIGHT

The DNA of a Successful Brand

"People believe in your brand because they believe in you. If there's a conflict between these two things, you will confuse the consumer because the two don't match."

-Merrilee Kick, Southern Champion

SUCCESSFUL BRANDS FIND GOOD PARTNERS

I'm a firm believer in collaboration and working with worthwhile partners. These joint ventures should be a win-win for all involved. And these relationships don't always have to be formal. Sometimes finding the right partner to further your brand and meet your initiatives is as close as your nearest Starbucks.

Jennifer Breen of SuiteHome says her relationship with the company has gone a long way in helping her provide excellent customer service to her customers.

"One of the best things we've ever done is co-brand with Starbucks. If you go to Starbucks.com, you can order personalized business cards which include a $5 Starbucks card. We give them out all the time with our business information, and I can't tell you the number of calls we get as a result.

If somebody is celebrating a work anniversary and we see it on LinkedIn, we celebrate them by sending them a Starbucks card with our business card on it. We will get an email back like, "Oh, we were just thinking about you. We have some stuff coming up in September." It happens all the time.

We order in bulk online from the corporate division of Starbucks, and it's a personal touch. People appreciate it.

It's one of the easiest things I've ever done. People love those little personalized tokens. It shows that we're thinking outside the box. Half the people we give them to are like, "We've never seen this before," and "Oh my gosh! This company is kind of cool, they think outside the box."

People like creative solutions to their problems and

when you do something clever or unique, you stand out; that's how you differentiate yourself.

We also have ones that say "Welcome!" We put them in the apartments when people get here, and half of our buildings have a Starbucks either downstairs or a block away. This simple act goes so far."

SUCCESSFUL BRANDS KNOW WHEN TO REBRAND

Kisa is an incredible purse designer here in Houston. I own three of her bags! When we first met at a pop-up shop a few years ago, I instantly fell in love with her work and I learned something about her brand that day. If you see it, buy it. She may not have another one like it! Kisa and I were at an event together recently and she shared she had just gone through a rebrand.

The Logo Confused Customers and Her Bank

Her first logo incorporated the elements she liked and reflected her target audience. It had her name and a circle. Her hand-sewn clutches are circles folded in half and she wanted that reflected in her logo.

The problem with the logo was that people kept trying to spell her name backward as reflected in her logo. It began to be a problem for her business (especially when trying to submit checks to the bank) so she opted to rebrand. She commissioned a designer to recreate her logo using the same elements—her name and circles.

Kisa shared that rebranding wasn't easy. Her clients were confused at first. They were looking for "KISA" spelled backward. Customers thought some new company was attempting to take over the designer's brand. Over time, Kisa's audience embraced the rebrand but she's not sure if she lost any potential customers along the way.

The Cost of a Rebrand

Traditionally, it has been quite expensive to rebrand a company and that still holds for many companies. Consider replacing signage if you have several locations or have a fleet of vehicles.

But in this digital age, rebranding for some companies can be done rather inexpensively. Such was the case for Jennifer Breen of SuiteHome.

"Our corporate clients in Chicago were begging us to expand. To oblige them, that meant rebranding and we were able to do a lot of that work internally. Since we've gone digital rebranding isn't as costly. A lot of our paper usage is gone. We do almost all e-leases and our invoicing is done electronically.

So, when we launched our rebrand, we hired an independent firm to handle our logos and graphics to keep things consistent. Once she designed the initial concept, we were able to execute it here in the office. Because our rebranding cost is relatively low, we refresh our logo about every three to four years.

The hardest or costliest thing we have to do is update or website. Our internal team handles all of our social media. It's a pretty quick process."

THE REBRANDING PROCESS IN THREE STEPS

If you've determined that your company name or logo are no longer relevant, consider rebranding.

If your business model has changed and you have new audience members, consider if rebranding is right for you. Gold Bond, a 111-year-old company, underwent a major rebrand to make itself relevant to a new generation of users.

Here are three things to remember during the rebranding process:

1. **Have a strategic plan.** Rebranding done wrong can cost you market share, and clients. Plus, your business could receive backlash from customers. Just ask the Gap.

2. **Communicate often.** Make internal and external customers aware of your rebranding efforts. Your

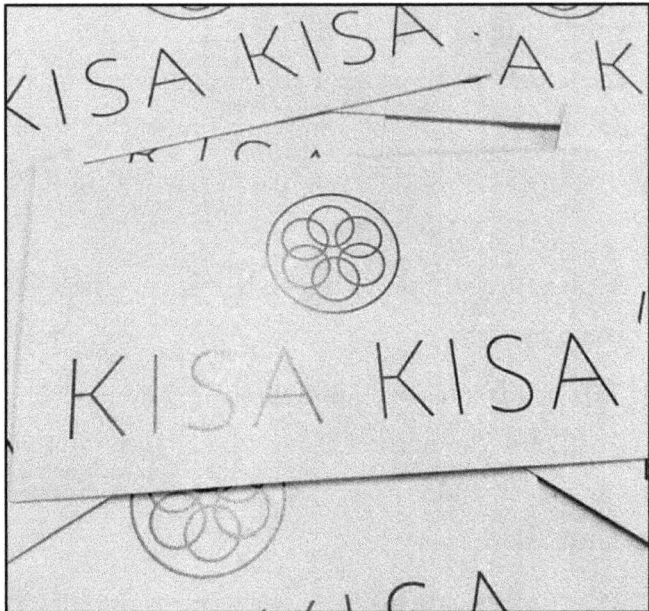

Top: Old logo. Bottom: New Logo. Courtesy of Kisa Williams

customers and employees want to be assured that the rebrand isn't going to cost them. Change isn't always easy or welcomed. Communicate your new mission and vision. Communicate the benefits. Communicate. Communicate. Communicate.

3. **Share the story.** If there's a good story behind the rebrand, share it. Kisa tied her sickle cell story to the rebrand. A good story helps audience members overcome objections and see the greater good in your brand. Now you're not simply rebranding for the sake of changing a logo. You're aligning your message with your core values in a more compelling way as to continue growth.

SUCCESSFUL BRANDS COMMUNICATE, CONNECT AND ARE CONSISTENT

To be consistent requires commitment, having the right tools, having the right people in place to utilize those tools and a good vision and mission statement to support it. Kathryn Freeland of A-TEK shares how she and her team execute all three.

> *"We have to work on brand consistency. It doesn't come naturally. It's not something that just happens. It's about how we communicate internally and so we have this mantra called "One team, One A-TEK,"–that means all of us working together to achieve one common goal.*

I'm conveying that message consistently and constantly—whether I'm communicating it directly in front of them, whether sending out newsletters or sending out memos. I'm constantly reiterating the 'One Team, One A-TEK' and explaining what that means.

If they feel like they're part of 'One Team, One A-TEK' and telling the customer, "You know what, I enjoy working for A-TEK because they come down here to see about us, and they send us stuff." That makes all the difference. That's branding and they may not realize that's what they're doing.

They are in front of the customer every day and if the customers are hearing positive things from the staff, then that translates into customer satisfaction and customer service. If employees are happy, the customers know that they're going to get the best out of the staff.

Conversely, sometimes the external branding can be difficult for companies. That's why we may not always have the pleasure to do full branding campaigns. So, we have to start with internal branding and then try to work our way external as much as we can."

SUCCESSFUL BRANDS SHARE GREAT STORIES

LaRose of Civil Engineering said she had difficulty convincing her engineers that they had a story to tell. She said typically engineers don't like to talk to people and this was a challenge at first. She designed their PowerPoint presentation with lots of pictures and very few words to urge engineers to tell the story, not spew out facts and figures. This change helped drive home why they were engineers in the first place.

She showed her team that they weren't, "just coming to work every day to do a job. It's more about why. We're making the community a better place."

Her advice to her engineers? "Get them to know that we are people too. Share stories about projects that you're passionate about because then they'll see and know your passion. They [clients] want to work with people that are passionate about what they're passionate about."

The new narrative at Civil Engineering is...Building Stronger Communities. "It's not just a road, it's a road that takes somebody to the hospital. It's more than just a road," LaRose shared.

SUCCESSFUL BRANDS ADHERE TO THE TEN COMMANDMENTS OF GOOD MARKETING

These are a few marketing truths that I've learned from helping clients market their business. It's what the million-dollar brands have echoed throughout this book.

1. To thine own target audience be true. Enough said.

2. Campaigns are not done until they've been tested. A/B testing is critical for any campaign whether it be an email campaign or advertising campaign. You need to know which version connects or resonates with your audience and then choose that version.

3. Use social media wisely. There are lots of examples of how not to do it. Make sure your business is counted among those that do it right.

4. Combine solid data, great images, and storytelling for best results.

5. Plan, set goals and be prepared for when stuff happens. People get sick, they forget due dates. Flights get canceled. Things get lost in the mail. The Internet goes down. Somebody rams their car into your building knocking out the power. Trust me. Stuff happens.

6. Email subject lines matter. This determines whether your email even gets opened and that's if it even lands in their inbox.

7. Great content is king, consistency is queen.

8. Say yes to engagement and no to content dumping.

9. Never forget your target audience. This bears repeating. It's easy to get caught up in our hype that we forget it's all about our target audience.

10. Good marketing produces measurable results.

SUCCESSFUL BRANDS SCAN THE HORIZON FOR OPPORTUNITIES

Many women business owners go through the certification process only to be disappointed that big businesses haven't lined-up at their door with big contracts. Kerrigan says that's not how the process works. She said, "Nobody tells you the tips and the tricks of the trade. It's not magic. You have to make the effort. You still have to show up." The wrong strategy according to Kerrigan is to get certified and then go to every big company out there and start filling out paperwork. She went on to say that it's a huge waste of time because those companies may not even be looking for your service or product. "Maybe they have an in-house agency, and they never go outside," she continued. Without a great deal of thought and research, the procurement process can leave many women business owners disappointed and depleted.

> *"At a recent procurement event, I learned something cool. A lady who worked in the metal scrapping business was there. Another woman who owned a company that provides wall coverings for hotels was also there. A big hotel chain was also there. Guess what? If you're the window covering business, the best time to reach out to the hotel is not when you know they're going to tear down their building in two months. But that is the right time for the scrap metal person to go in and begin a conversation.*
>
> *It confirmed for me that you have to do your research and understand how your being at an event makes sense. You have to approach these companies at the right time. You have to stalk them to know the right time to approach."*

FINAL THOUGHTS

In marketing, there is no one-size-fits-all. One approach or methodology does not work across all industries or meet all goals.

These million-dollar brands understand that establishing your culture, mission, values, and goals is a must, knowing your target audience is key. Also, excellent customer service is a non-negotiable and understanding that your most important resource—the human one—can make or break your brand.

Now, how you communicate and engage your target audience will vary from industry-to-industry.

And that's what million-dollar brands know and now, so do you.

ABOUT THE AUTHOR

Known as The Marketing Stylist™, Lisa N. Alexander has worked as an art director, graphic designer and marketing director throughout her 20-plus year career. As a consultant, and owner of PrettyWork Creative LLC and PrettyWork Studios, she helps small business owners grow their businesses through strategic marketing, branding and effective storytelling.

Lisa describes this process as helping clients develop their WOW factor for their big marketing red carpet events and her clients love her for this.

Taking the storytelling process to a new level, Lisa and her husband Elgin Alexander produced their first documentary entitled, What Mercy Looks Like. It is a story about the volunteers who helped to rebuild Houston after Hurricane Harvey and the organization who spearheaded the mission. The documentary won a Gold Remi at the 2018 WorldFest Houston International Independent Film Festival and was selected for screening at the 2018 San Antonio Film Festival.

One of Lisa's greatest achievements was going back to school and graduating with honors from Ashford University with a B.A. in PR and Marketing.

She's also very proud of her volunteer work. Lisa has volunteered at Freedom Place — a safe house for young girls rescued from sex trafficking. Lisa served on the City of Houston's Women and Minority Owned Business Taskforce. Lisa was also the board secretary for Get Together Northwest Houston and has served on the National Association of Women Business Owners (NAWBO) Houston board as Director of Public Relations and is the current Chapter President.

Lisa is available for speaking opportunities and marketing consulting; connect with her at lisanalexander.com.

REFERENCES

Introduction

Nathanson, Jon, (November 14, 2013). "The Economics of Infomercials." Pricenomics. Retrieved from: https://priceonomics.com/the-economics-of-infomercials/

Isola, Abram, (May 29, 2018). "31 Essential Direct Mail Marketing Automation Stats You Need to Know." Inkit. Retrieved from: https://inkit.io/2018/05/31-essential-direct-mail-marketing-automation-statistics/

To Thine Ownself Be True: Why Defining Your Company's Vision, Mission & Personality Matters

King, Shaun, (October 23, 2011). "3 Hard-Earned Lessons and Why I Resigned." Church Leaders. Retrieved from: https://churchleaders.com/pastors/pastor-how-to/154215-shaun_king_3_extemely_hard-earned_lessons_on_starting_something_new_change_and_discipleship.html

Branding, Culture and Customer Service

Gabor, Deb. (2017, July 26). The 12 Brand Archetypes: Which One Are You? Success.com. Retrieved July 06, 2019, from https://www.success.com/the-12-brand-archetypes-which-one-are-you/

Yohn, Denise Lee, (2017, July 11). 9 Different Types of Brands [Web log post]. Retrieved July 06, 2019, from https://deniseleeyohn. com/9-different-types-of-brands/

Kerr, Dara. "Uber's U-Turn: How the New CEO Is Cleaning House after Scandals and Lawsuits." C|Net, 27 Apr. 2018, www.cnet.com/news/ubers-u-turn-how-ceo-dara-khosrowshahi-is-cleaning-up-after-scandals-and-lawsuits/.

Fowler, Susan, (2017, February 19). Reflecting On One Very, Very Strange Year At Uber [Web log post]. Retrieved from https:// www.susanjfowler.com/blog/2017/2/19/ reflecting-on-one-very-strange-year-at-uber

Customer Service and the Bottom Line [Audio blog interview]. (2014, March 6). Retrieved from https://lisanalexander.com/ podcast-customer-service-and-the-bottom-line/

Hiring Your First Employee [Audio blog interview]. (2014, January 9). Retrieved from https://lisanalexander. com/shoptalk-ep-12-bes-hiring-first-employee/

Traditional vs. Digital Marketing — The Many Ways to Market Your Business

Lister, Mary, (June 9, 2019). "37 Staggering Video Marketing Statistics for 2018." Word Stream. Retrieved from: https://www.wordstream.com/blog/

ws/2017/03/08/video-marketing-statistics

Media, (September 17, 2013). "Under the Influence: Consumer Trust in Advertising." Nielsen. Retrieved from: https://www.nielsen.com/us/en/insights/news/2013/under-the-influence-consumer-trust-in-advertising.html

Adaptive, (March 5, 2014). "How Social Media Amplifies the Power of Word-of-mouth." Incite Group. Retrieved from: http://www.usefulsocialmedia.com/brand-marketing/how-social-media-amplifies-power-word-mouth

30 Fast Facts about Video [Web log post]. (n.d.). Retrieved from https://www.wyzowl.com/30-amazing-facts-about-video/

Video will account for an overwhelming majority of internet traffic by 2021. (2017, June 12). Business Insider. Retrieved from https://www.businessinsider.com/heres-how-much-ip-traffic-will-be-video-by-2021-2017-6

Millennials depend on word-of-mouth more than Boomers. (2014, January 21). Retrieved from https://www.retailwire.com/discussion/millennials-depend-on-word-of-mouth-more-than-boomers/

Miller, Grace, (n.d.). 38 Referral Marketing Statistics That Will Make You Want To Start A RAF Program Tomorrow. Retrieved from https://www.annexcloud.

com/blog/39-referral-marketing-statistics-that-will-make-you-want-to-start-a-raf-program-tomorrow/

Leveraging PR, Sponsorship Opportunities, Promotional Items and Appointments

Sternberg, Josh, (November 30, 2017). "Is Sending Out a Press Release Really Worth the Money?" Entrepreneur. Retrieved from: https://www.entrepreneur.com/article/304383

Employees Are Brand Ambassadors: Hire the Right People

Morgan, Blake, (2017, September 25). Customer Service Is A $350 Billion Industry, And It's A Mess. Forbes. Retrieved from https://www.forbes.com/sites/blakemorgan/2017/09/25/customer-service-is-a-350b-industry-and-its-a-mess/#30b118c011be

Goltz, Jay, (2012, April 10). Why Small Businesses Fail to Grow. The New York Times. Retrieved from https://boss.blogs.nytimes.com/2012/04/10/why-small-businesses-fail-to-grow/